Historical Israel:
Biblical Israel

Mark Harris

The Cassell Biblical Studies Series

SERIES EDITOR: STEVE MOYISE

The Cassell Biblical Studies Series is aimed at those taking a course of biblical studies. Developed for the use of those embarking on theological and ministerial education, it is equally helpful in local church situations, and for lay people confused by apparently conflicting approaches to the Scriptures.

Students of biblical studies today will encounter a diversity of interpretive positions. Their teachers will – inevitably – lean towards some positions in preference to others. This series offers an integrated approach to the Bible which recognizes this diversity, but helps readers to understand it, and to work towards some kind of unity within it.

This is an ecumenical series, written by Roman Catholics and Protestants. The writers are all professionally engaged in the teaching of biblical studies in theological and ministerial education. The books are the product of that experience, and it is the intention of the editor, Dr Steve Moyise, that their contents should be tested on this exacting audience.

ALREADY PUBLISHED:

Introduction to Biblical Studies
Steve Moyise

FORTHCOMING TITLES INCLUDE:

Jesus and The Gospels
Clive Marsh and Steve Moyise

Historical Israel:
Biblical Israel

Studying Joshua to 2 Kings

MARY E. MILLS

CASSELL

Cassell
Wellington House, 125 Strand, London WC2R 0BB
370 Lexington Avenue, New York, NY 10017–6550
www.cassell.co.uk

First published 1999

British Library Cataloguing-in-Publication Data
A catalogue record for this book is available from the British Library.

ISBN 0-304-70474-1

Quotes are from *The Revised Standard Version* of the Bible, © 1946,
1952, 1971 by the Division of Christian Education of the National
Council of the Churches of Christ in the USA. Used by permission.

Typeset by SetSystems Ltd, Saffron Walden, Essex
Printed and bound in Great Britain by
Biddles Ltd, Guildford and King's Lynn

Contents

Acknowledgements

The research for this book has been carried out alongside a normal teaching schedule; it has, therefore, taken nearly a year since the idea of the volume came to mind to complete the text. As the months have gone past the subject of historical and biblical Israel has become an old friend and a constant companion and I am grateful for the invitation to delve into the Deuteronomistic histories.

I wish to express my gratitude to the Research Committee of St Mary's University College who provided me with a much-needed grant towards books for my work, and also to my patient reader, Anne Laing Brooks, whose enthusiasm and untiring attention to the presentation of the material has greatly aided this project.

Mary E. Mills
April 1998

Foreword

The so-called 'historical' books of the Old Testament from Joshua to Kings are important for several different reasons. Most obviously, they are a potential source of information about the history of ancient Israel, from its settlement in the land of Canaan down to the Exile to Babylonia in the sixth century BC. But even a cursory reading shows that they are not, as they stand, a neutral or purely factual history. Like the historiography of any other nation, these books reflect the concerns and interests of their authors. Without a study of these interests it is not possible to understand them properly, and so to extract what historical information they really contain. Furthermore, the question of the intentions of the authors is interesting in its own right, for these books are part of the literature of ancient Israel. Some parts at least of the histories amount to literature of a high order: we remember so many of the stories in Judge or Samuel because they are so well written, whatever their relationship to sober historical fact. By reading between the lines we may also discover much about the social realities of life in Israel; and, last but not least, we can trace the theological concerns that animated those who compiled the histories.

Until now it has been difficult to find a book which concentrated equally on all four of these aspects: historical, literary, sociological, and theological. One major contribution of Mary Mills's work is to hold these four things in equal balance. Her book will be of interest to those primarily wanting to know about the history of Israel, but also to those who want to read the historical books as literary masterpieces or to trace their social and theologica concerns. In all four areas there has been a work of major importance in the last decade, and this account is fully up to date and thoroughly well informed about them all. It makes current scholarship accessible to a wider audience, and provides an excellent introduction to the study of the Old Testament in general by its reader-friendly approach. I hope it will be very widely read and used.

John Barton
Oriel & Lang Professor of the Interpretation of Holy Scripture,
University of Oxford

1

Introduction

The title of this book indicates its twofold purpose – to examine the literary account of Israel's history to be found in the books of Joshua, Judges, 1 and 2 Samuel and 1 and 2 Kings and to investigate how far these accounts form 'the history of Israel'. In the Hebrew Bible, Joshua to 2 Kings are known as the Former Prophets; the book of Ruth, which in the English Bible is found between Judges and 1 Samuel, is in the third, Writings, section of the Hebrew Bible. The term 'Israel' is used frequently in the Old Testament (OT) to denote the people chosen by the God of Israel (whose personal name is YHWH; rendered 'Yahweh' in some English translations and 'the LORD' in others) and the Land which their God gave them to dwell in. It is known outside the biblical record in an inscription engraved on a stone pillar called by archaeologists the 'Merneptah Stele'. This carries a record of victories won by an Egyptian ruler in the region of Palestine in the thirteenth century BCE; it includes a reference to Israel as a people or land, rather than a city. From this it is clear that Israel existed as a social unit in the ancient world, but the reference is a passing one and does not give any details of who or what constituted Israel at that time.

The question can then be raised; 'How far is the biblical account of Israel to be read as a documentary account of the past and what does it tell the reader about the development of an ancient society?' The books from Joshua to 2 Kings give an account of how Israel came into the Land, by conquest, and how the Land was divided up between the twelve tribes. Leadership was at first offered by Joshua and then by judges, before the apointment of kings. At the death of Saul, the first king, David united northern and southern tribes in one national alliance. But after the death of his successor, King Solomon, north and south divided again and there were two separate states of Israel (the north) and Judah (the south). At the end of the monarchical period first Israel and then Judah were overwhelmed by invasions from the north, resulting in the disappearance of Israelite and Judahite society as independent national states. This historical narrative, however, is continually told from a religious perspective; in many ways the main actor on the stage is the invisible, but all-powerful, God of Israel.

This opens up two ways of evaluating the text, as history and as theology. Israel in the first context is a nation living in the northern highlands of Palestine from the late second millennium BCE to the mid-sixth century BCE. In the second setting Israel is a people defined by its religion, especially by its relationship to its patron deity. These two contexts may be interpreted together or they may be explored as separate elements.

Historical Israel

The books from Joshua to 2 Kings have an historical framework, but that in turn is conditioned by the overall shaping of the OT. The OT is a collection of many individual works but these are grouped into sections by the Hebrew Bible, the original language version of the material. In the first section there are five books of Law (Torah). The contents of these are set out in chronological order, starting with creation of the universe, of human beings, the nations and finally Israel. The origins of Israel are found in the founding fathers or patriarchs – Abraham, Isaac, Jacob. In the Exodus from Egypt, led by Moses, the Israelites turn into an independent people; in their encounter with YHWH in the desert, at the holy mountain of Sinai, they gained a way of life, both civil and religious, as set out in the Ten Commandments and other laws. The last law book, that of Deuteronomy, tells of Moses' final speeches to the people of Israel and of his death.

Joshua follows on from this since it deals with what happened after the death of Moses and how the divine promises of land were fulfilled. This in turn opens the way for the stages of history outlined above. The narrative of Joshua to 2 Kings then, is part of a longer perspective in the OT which situates the nation of Israel in the history of the development of ancient societies. Continuity of material is ensured since the same God presides over all the events dealt with.

The story of biblical Israel is set within a geographical area which actually exists and which can be explored, so it is possible to evaluate the biblical setting of Israel from modern archaeological

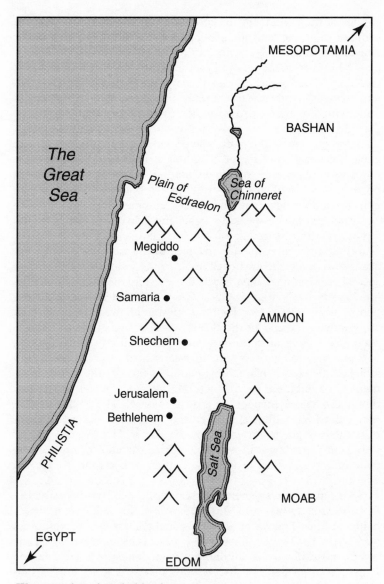

Water and ancient habitation

Coastal plains receive best of Mediterranean storms.

Water least available on eastern slopes of central highlands.

Ancient habitation found in coastal cities and in fortress cities such as Megiddo which control north–south passes.

Trade routes are north–south via coastal plains and passes.

studies of the region. In this context it may be useful to establish some of the basic facts about its physical setting. The area under consideration is a long, narrow strip of land, bounded on the west by the Mediterranean Sea and on the east by mountains and desert (see map). The natural routes through the region lie north–south and connect it with two much more significant land areas to north and south. In the north two major rivers, Tigris and Euphrates, provided resources for powerful civilizations in Mesopotamia, while, in the south, the river Nile provided the foundation for the ancient civilization of Egypt. The long strip of land between these two major regions of human habitation formed a corridor from north to south and was, therefore, prized both by Mesopotamian cultures and by Egypt, as part of their empires.

Although the OT speaks of Israel and Canaan as names for the region, modern historians of the ancient world prefer to label it Syro-Palestine, allowing for the fact that a number of different groups occupied the area over time. In the Late Bronze Age (late second millennium) Egypt was the overlord of the area and its local rulers were kings of city states which had no real independence. The collapse of Egyptian power allowed a measure of autonomy at the end of the Bronze Age, but this appears to have been also a time of destabilization with small city states fighting one another, followed by the invasions of the Sea Peoples who attacked the coastal plain. This period of time marks the development of habitation in the central highlands which is usually thought to be evidence for the growth of Israel. The power vacuum may indeed have allowed local rulers the space for expansion, but this was brought to an end with the rise of Neo-Assyria and of Babylonia in the eighth to sixth centuries BCE and the consequent invasion of Israel and Judah and their submission to foreign empires.

Syro-Palestine was, then, an area of only moderate possibilities in economic terms, and this determined its political status of being in the shadow of neighbouring regions whose resources were greater. Only at times when these cultures were in decline did the possibility of an autonomous state emerge. Even then, the kingdoms of Israel and Judah only governed a section of Palestine, surrounded by other nations and with part of the coast governed by the Philistines (Sea Peoples). The lack of abundant water and good soil meant that Palestinian society could not rival those lands watered by great rivers. Early habitation appears to have focused on the western plain, with the highlands being developed only after the skills of cistern making emerged, allowing for the cultivation of soil in the dry months, with the aid of land terracing.

It is into this land that the Israelites came after the Exodus, according to the OT, and the accounts of Israel and Judah in Joshua to 2 Kings describe life in this area. The narratives, however, are set into the perspective of Israelite interests, with the land defined as 'The Land', the one promised by God to his people. In this context Israel serves as a name both for a people and for a physical area. Other peoples in Syro-Palestine are labelled by the generic term 'Canaan' and are viewed as outsiders and as opponents. The major divide is that of religion. What defines Israel is its monotheistic worship of its deity; Canaanites have a polytheistic system which is alien to Israel and which Israel's God opposes. The Canaanites are destined to be overcome by Israel, provided that it remains monotheistic.

Thus the basics of historical geography are coloured by a religious message which is aimed at the readers of the OT, who the text implicitly assumes will be sympathetic to this. What emerges in the books of the OT is biblical Israel, the Israel created by the text.

Biblical Israel

'Israel' is a key term in the OT. Jacob is re-named Israel in Genesis 32 and is the father of twelve sons from whom are formed twelve tribes, the tribes of Israel. Jacob/Israel go down to Egypt and are set free from slavery there to travel to the desert to meet with their God. This is the first time that the whole nation had contact with its patron deity. The meeting at Sinai forges a national system of values and cult which is to be taken up by Israel once it enters its Land. These events are linked back to distant ancestors and to the origins of the universe. Such is the content of 'Israel' in Torah; a national identity is created here.

In the second section of the Hebrew Scriptures, that of Prophecy (Nebi'im), the reader discovers what happens when Israel crosses the Jordan and settles in Canaan: how it establishes control of its land, and how different forms of leadership emerge. The message of disaster which the writing prophets announce is addressed to Israel and Judah as societies, and particularly to the upper classes of those societies. The life of Israel comes to an end with the Assyrian and Babylonian invasions and the Exile. Those who are said to return from the Exile are no longer 'Israelites' but 'Jews', a name given to them by their captors on account of their

homeland and of their language, for they are men of Judah and
speak its language. From Judah and Judahite comes a new foundation for 'Israelite' identity.

The Hebrew Scriptures create a detailed picture of what constitutes Israel. At the heart of this is religious practice of worship.
Israel worships YHWH because that God controls its life; having
chosen Abraham and his wife, God made them founding parents
of a chosen nation. Not only did YHWH choose this nation for
himself he made himself known to them, calling them into a
covenant contract relationship. Hosea 11 describes Israel as God's
son and pictures God as a parent nurturing his child. Thus Israel
becomes God's family. This profile of biblical Israel clearly bears
some relationship to historical Israel, but it presents a picture in
which slow developments have been speeded up, as with the
settlement of the land, and material has been harmonized to give
a single narrative, as with the cycles of short stories about different
local leaders in Judges.

The OT, then, provides a literary and religious account of
Israel, not in the form of a theological treatise but in the form of a
record of human life. The central part of this account is to be
found in Joshua to 2 Kings. Each text in this section has its own
content but taken together the texts record a new phase in the
social and political development of Israel. So are these works the
product of different authors or is one mastermind at work here,
gathering into a continuous account material from many sources?
It has been noted, with regard to Joshua to 2 Kings, that they not
only tell a continuous story but that there is a continuity of
vocabulary and outlook between these books and between them
and the book of Deuteronomy. M. Noth described these books,
therefore, as the Deuteronomistic Histories, a title not known in
the OT (or to Judaism, which calls these books the Former
Prophets) but now usually employed by modern scholarship. By
this title Noth highlighted the overall coherence of the texts and
the manner in which their many separate stories have been woven
into a continuum in which all events refer back to the overarching
power of the God of Israel.

The Deuteronomistic Histories

Noth's argument is that wherever the material for the books Joshua
to 2 Kings came from originally, it is now sewn together in a
continuous account which provides a common theme and offers
the reader a focal point from which to view the history of Israel.

This common theme is in line with the theology of the book of Deuteronomy. This book lays down a blueprint for Israel's future lifestyle in the Land. The Land is YHWH's gift, and so the life of the people must focus on that one God and on doing his will. There is one deity and one central sanctuary for worship, just as there is one nation which acts as a just and fair society in everyday internal affairs and which has an established cultic code. In chapter 28 Moses offers his audience a glimpse of the future. If they abide by the teaching in Deuteronomy they will have blessing in the Land, but if they worship other gods they will be cursed. The text dwells on the sufferings such a curse would entail, as though the writer already knows that disaster has befallen Israel.

This opens the way for regarding Deuteronomy as the first, introductory work of the Histories which follow, rather than describing it as the last book of the Torah. With knowledge of Deuteronomy in mind, the reader is then led to follow the actions of Israel in living out the promises and the sorrows predicted there. What the great heroes and leaders do is always balanced against the over-arching control of YHWH. When the kings of Israel and Judah lead their people into worshipping a variety of deities they are doomed and the nations with them. This line of sin and judgement is seen most clearly in 2 Kings, but there are traces of it throughout the books. Noth argued that there was a school of thinkers and writers who worked on older folk stories and archives to piece together their account of the real meaning of the past and so give meaning to the present. Noth thought that they were operating in the late monarchy in Judah and in the Exile. This is partly due to the reference in Kings to the finding of an old Lawbook in the Jersualem Temple in the time of King Josiah (2 Kings 22). Scholars have argued that this is the historical finding of Deuteronomy, a find which led to religious reform in the direction of a more focused Yahvism. (the religion of the God, YaHWeH). Those who advocated such reform formed a coherent group at court, the Deuteronomists. Later on, after the Exile, another edition of Israelite history was produced by the Chronicler (1 and 2 Chronicles). This version adapted the earlier Deuteronomistic History to meet new interests among the Judahite elite.

Recently this view has been challenged by G. Auld, who disputes the sequence of Deuteronomist and Chronicler. In his book *Kings Without Privilege*, Auld argues that the two versions of the past should be viewed as parallel editions of older source material where they deal with the same subject-matter. This is particularly relevant to the history of the kings from David to the end of the monarchy. He works through the stories of kings in both Histories, setting out that which he considers to be the material common to both and on which both works equally depend. This allows the reader to examine the manner in which each version of the original has added to or changed this older account. Auld warns the reader against the assumption that a book which seems to take a practical attitude to events (the Deuteronomistic History) should be set up as older than a text which takes a more idealistic view of affairs (the Chronicler's History). In Auld's view these approaches can emerge simultaneously. Auld considers both Histories to have come from the exilic time which lessens the value of the reference in 2 Kings to Josiah and the ancient Lawbook. However he argues for some connection with the reforming movements of the end of the Judahite monarchy by suggesting a link between the prophet Jeremiah and the book of Kings (Auld, 1994, p. 169).

Conclusions

The existence of two versions of the same material alerts the reader to the fact that even in modern times, with the pursuit of scientific truth, the story of the past is inevitably mediated through the mind of the contemporary researcher. Different interpretations of the past stand side by side in the OT, and the modern reader can only view historical events through their separate lenses and attempt to work out what purpose the writers of each account had in mind. Different twentieth-century readers then produce independent and even opposing theories concerning the origins and relationship of the ancient books. It is not easy in modern historical research to agree on the criteria by which a piece of historical evidence is judged to be an accurate or truthful representation of events. The task of defining the historical value of the Deuteronomistic texts for an ancient audience is even more complicated, since the ancient world did not have a modern 'scientific' attitude to accounts of the past. Whereas a modern researcher tries to 'tell it as it was' with regard to the words and actions of key persons, the editors of OT material may well have been more concerned with passing on overarching religious traditions, thus maintaining the link between past and present, with less attention to historical details.

What enlightenment, then, has been offered to the reader concerning the title *Historical Israel: Biblical Israel*? It is clear that the concept of Israel cannot be pinned down to any one meaning. Rather it carries a number of related meanings with regard to the

OT library of books. On the one hand there certainly was a historical society called Israel which lived in the central highlands of Syro-Palestine, and modern archaeological research can help to uncover what sort of society that was. The OT is ultimately the product of this society, produced in its existing form late in the life of Israelite/Judahite culture. However, the biblical account of the history of Israel is in many ways a separate entity from the historical and geographical reality. 'Biblical Israel' is a theological construct, a people defined as a congregation of worshippers, in relation to their patron deity. To this extent the Deuteronomistic Histories are theological works having religious truth as their goal. This biblical Israel is set out through literary forms and the message concerning it is shaped by the narratives which convey that message to the reader. To that extent the History is a piece of literature like others and can be studied through the discipline of literary analysis.

In the rest of this book these three strands of the concept of 'historical Israel,' will be pursued. The first section of the book will examine issues connected with the link between text and history, taking three main debates as they impinge on particular sections of the Deuteronomistic History. The second section will turn to the role of history as narrative and the manner in which literary examinations of the text reveal further layers of interest to the modern reader, particularly in the area of women's contributions to events in the public life of a society. The third section will turn to theological themes which emerge across the History as a whole, looking back to Deuteronomy as foundational in this regard.

Historical Issues

2

Joshua and the conquest of Canaan

Following models set out in the Introduction to this book, the text of Joshua can be described as the first book in the Prophecy section of the Hebrew Bible or as the first of the Deuteronomistic Histories. In this chapter the latter model will be taken up. As the first stage in a longer history of Israel in the Land, Joshua sets the scene for the ultimate development of Israel as a nation with its own territory. But it is necessary to look back to previous events in the life of Israel as well, in order to situate the text fully.

In Deuteronomy the people of Israel have already become a great nation on the move. Having grown into a separate nation in Egypt, Israel has been allowed, finally, to depart from there to meet with its God in the wilderness. There in the desert they have been told by God what is expected of them as God's chosen people. At the start of Deuteronomy Moses reminds Israel of its past and looks to a future in the Promised Land, the territory which will be given it by its patron God. If Israel keeps all the laws and commandments of God set out in chapters 12 to 26 of the book it will live at peace in the Land and will experience prosperity there. Part of this law is the eradication of the nations already occupying the Land, by violent conquest. It is this conquest which the first eleven chapters of Joshua describe.

The story of the conquest

The book of Joshua opens with the death of Moses, whose role as leader is now taken up by Joshua son of Nun. God tells Joshua that he is to take the people into the Land; thus the divine promises will be fulfilled. Scenes follow in quick succession – the river is crossed and the whole male population of Israel committed to God in the ritual of circumcision. They are now ready to invade the Land, which they do, taking Jericho and Ai and defeating the Amorites. By chapter 12 the whole Land has fallen to the Israelites. It remains to divide up the newly-acquired territory among the twelve tribes, a topic which occupies chapters 13 to 19. The last chapters turn to the completion of Joshua's task and the coming of death. Before he dies, Joshua gathers the whole people together to a ceremony of renewal of their commitment to the God who has fought for them and brought them success in the wars with local kings.

This, then, is the account of conquest given in Joshua and read by modern readers as the history of Israel's past migration. But is this modern history writing? Certain features of the story should give the reader pause for thought. The Land is described as a large territory and as filled with inhabitants. Yet only a few battles and sieges are described in detail, and these appear to operate as set pieces which suffice for the whole, lengthy campaign. Other events of the wars are passed over quickly, using a repeating formula, as in chapter 10, verses 29–43. There are several versions of the giving out of the Land, set side by side in the middle of the book and not fully harmonized with each other; chapter 13 gives one version whereas chapters 14–18 give another. At the end of the work also there are different versions of the story of how Joshua called Israel together, in chapters 23 and 24. These repetitions indicate that the writer was aware of more than one tradition about this material and that, rather than produce one, 'true' version, he preferred to record the variety of information available. It is still possible to see the variety within the text even though there has been some harmonization on the editor's part.

Furthermore Joshua shows signs of a formalized manner of story-telling. The crossing of the river deliberately echoes the earlier Israelite crossing of the Sea of Reeds, with the people passing through unscathed. The waters of the Jordan pile up to either side of the column of people in chapter 3, only returning to their course when Israel has passed through. Joshua tells the people to pass on the meaning of this event to their children. 'For the Lord your God dried up the waters of the Jordan for you until you passed over, as the Lord your God did to the Red Sea' (Josh 4:23). The Ark of the Lord plays a major part in this miracle and continues to bring divine assistance to Israel when it leads the people into battle. The fall of Jericho, for instance, is told as a miracle story in which the carrying out of appropriate ritual causes the walls of the city to collapse. Later on the men of Gibeon are defeated in a great battle which oversets the normal run of sun and moon. 'Then spoke Joshua to the Lord . . . And the sun stood still, and the moon stayed, until the nation took vengeance on their enemies' (Josh 10:12–13). These points lead to the conclusion that Joshua was not intended to be a scientific account of the invasion of Canaan, but rather a theological narrative which reflects religious traditions about the past and which stresses the central role of the Lord of Israel in the events of national life.

Historical background

The question then arises as to how these religious accounts of events are to be reconciled with 'what really happened'. It would, for instance, be possible to argue that Joshua provides a religious account of events which nevertheless is very close to the original. This would lead to the view that it is correct to describe Israel as a nation formed outside Palestine which invaded that land and replaced existing culture and religion with a specifically Israelite version, as was indeed, argued by scholars such as W. F. Albright in the first half of the twentieth century.

One modern manner of validating historical material is to compare stories of the same event taken from different sources. Unfortunately it is not possible to use this method with the OT, since there are no known Israelite accounts of the past outside the biblical account. So far archaeologists have not found any inscriptions on stone or written texts on papyrus, parchment or clay, which would support or challenge the evidence from the Bible with regard to the settlement of Palestine. The only possible resource is archaeological evidence of a more general nature. The remains of cities in Palestine form large hills (tells) which can be excavated layer by layer. Scholars working on this material have found no evidence for a swift invasion of Palestine at the appropriate time period (see chart). V. Fritz, for instance, states 'The decline of Canaanite urban culture remains so far largely unexplained. It is certain only that the occupation of the land by the Israelites . . . was not the *cause* but the *result* of this breakdown' (Fritz, 1994, p. 116). Jericho, it appears, was destroyed two hundred years or so before the arrival of Israel according to biblical chronology. The cities excavated show no sign of consistent destruction at the same date and there is no immediate change in house architecture or in styles of domestic pottery ware – both of them signs of cultural innovations in an area.

What is to be made of this evidence? It has to be said that the biblical account of conquest is the projection backwards of the

Table of dating for ancient Syro-Palestine

Neolithic	8000–4000 BCE	
Chalcolithic	4000–3150	
Early Bronze Age 1	3150–2950	
Early Bronze Age 2	2950–2650	
Early Bronze Age 3	2650–2350	
Early Bronze Age 4	2350–2150	
Middle Bronze Age 1	2150–1950	Approximate dating for patriarchal stories
Middle Bronze Age 2A	1950–1750	
Middle Bronze Age 2B	1750–1550	
Late Bronze Age 1	1550–1400	Possible date for biblical exodus
Late Bronze Age 2	1400–1200	
Iron Age 1	1200–1000	Rise of biblical kingdom of Israel
Iron Age 2A	1000–900	David, Solomon, divided kingdoms
Iron Age 2B	900–700	Rise of Assyria, conquest of Samaria
Iron Age 2C	700–587	Rise of Babylonia, fall of Jerusalem
Iron Age 3	587–332	Babylonian and Persian Empires rule Palestine
Hellenistic Period	332–37	
Roman Period	37 BCE–324 CE	

The overall chronology of the Bronze Age in Palestine is based on Egyptian chronology because enough traces of Egyptian influence on Palestinian life have survived to make it possible to integrate Palestine with an Egyptian timeframe.

(Table based on V. Fritz, *An Introduction to Biblical Archaeology* (Sheffield, 1994)).

---

understanding of its past held by a later age. This projecting back of current ideas has the effect of harmonizing and compressing events which originally marked a slower and more gradual transition from Late Bronze Age society to Iron Age culture. The emergence of this picture from recent developments in biblical archaeology has led to a number of differing opinions among scholars about what actually happened. Some of these opinions will now be examined.

Scholarly views

The general range of possibilities has been summarised by V. Fritz:

- a conquest of Canaanite cities by Israelite tribes (Albright)
- peaceful occupation of the land by nomads in the course of changing pasture-grounds (Alt)
- the revolutionary uprising of the lower classes and replacement of the ruling population by a new society (Mendenhall)
  (Fritz, 1994, p. 137)

The first possibility was held by W. F. Albright in the late 1940s when biblical archaeology had not examined so many sites and it was not possible to point to facts such as that Jericho did not appear to have been destroyed in the Late Bronze Age. The increasing amount of knowledge of ancient Palestinian sites has led scholars to abandon a simple harmonization of material evidence with the biblical narrative, and to adapt biblical narrative to 'on the ground' evidence. A. Alt adjusted the picture, therefore, to allow for increasing migration by nomadic groups who entered Palestine gradually over many years and slowly came to settle there, displacing groups already in possession of land. This version still accepts that groups from outside Palestine were the major cause of change. Mendenhall's version has been more generally adopted. He argues for a radical shift of peoples within the land, as well as some immigration. Urban society came under pressure from several sources, towns became unstable and vulnerable places, leaving a new economic focus to emerge among pastoral peoples living in the central highlands.

A recent book by N. P. Lemche (Lemche, 1988) brings together the general framework of the biblical account and the details drawn from archaeological reconstructions. The main focus of the biblical account is the emergence of Israel as a nation in Palestine. This brief frame can be filled in from archaeology as follows:

1. Gradual collapse of Late Bronze Age society and the city states of Canaan. The evidence for this collapse comes from the Amarna Letters which were found in the abandoned city of the deposed Pharaoh Akhnaten, and which record the struggles of dependent Canaanite rulers to keep order in Canaan. In these letters there are references to guerilla groups called 'Apiru' (regarded by many as the source of the name Hebrews). These roaming bands of unsettled armed men may have been a focus for the newly developing population centres in the hills.

2. Internal feuds/Upheaval in Egypt (the Egyptians dominated Palestine in the Late Bronze Age)/the arrival and settlement of Philistines on the coast by Gaza.
3. These all led to internal migration from the plains to the more secure land in the central highlands.
4. Increased permanent habitation of the central highlands. This took the form of tribal society dependent on pasturing animals and growing some grain crops. These tribal groups lived in small villages. Latest surveys by the archaeologist Finkelstein show the increase of numbers of such settlements in the early Iron Age (Finkelstein, 1988).

Lemche fills out the details of this picture of the growth of Israel in chapter three of his book. While acknowledging archaeology, it also gives credence to the essential fact that Israel was an individual culture and society. However, Israel here emerges within Canaan; it is one aspect of Palestinian society and not totally separate from this base. Its culture and religion are to be viewed in continuity with other local Palestinian cultures.

The construction of history

This idea of a continuum between Israel and Canaan is, of course, very different from the perspective offered in the Deuteronomistic Histories which portray Canaanite culture as foreign and opposed to Israel's practices. K. Whitelam's book *The Invention of Ancient Israel* (1996) is an extended discussion of precisely this kind of issue. Whitelam argues that since the rise of modern biblical criticism the biblical account has consistently been interpreted through the eyes of Western European thinkers. There has been a bias overall to acknowledging modern Europe's inheritance from the Bible, mediated through Christianity. Israel needs to represent 'the West' rather than 'the Orient', and that is achieved by accepting literally biblical cultural symbols. This literal acceptance of the OT's presentation of the past was endorsed through the application of western scientific history to the ancient literature – a task made possible in the first stages of the rise of biblical archaeology. 'Israel' can then be lifted out from the text and created anew according to the cultural needs of a Western perspective. Whitelam points out that Alt, for instance, wrote his version of Israel's emergence against the background of contemporary twentieth-century developments in Palestine, with the increase of Zionist immigration into the area:

The central feature of Alt's construction, significant immigration of groups in search of a national homeland, needs to be considered in the context of these dramatic developments in Palestine at the time he was conducting his research . . . (Whitelam, 1996, p. 76)

In Whitelam's view none of the three main theories on the origins of Israel – conquest, migration or revolution – can survive the evidence for a specifically Palestinian, or, in biblical language, Canaanite development. Israel was inherently a part of regional geography and politics and did not result from an imposition of a totally separate culture from outside:

> The driving force of biblical studies has been the need to search for ancient Israel as the taproot of western civilisation . . . Biblical scholarship, in its all-consuming search for ancient Israel, has reflected the myopia of the West in general, and the early Zionists in particular, in ignoring the indigenous population and its claims to the land or the past. (Whitelam, 1996, p. 119)

Another work, that of P. R. Davies, *In Search of Ancient Israel*, (1992), has attacked the view that the account of Israel in the OT is the same reality as actual historical Israel. Davies wishes to argue that the picture of historic Israel in the OT is that promulgated in the post-exilic province of Yehud (Judah) in the Persian Empire (fifth–fourth centuries BCE). He begins his book by delineating three Israels – biblical, historical and ancient Israel. This last, he says, is a total fiction created by modern scholarship which has harmonized biblical Israel with aspects of archaeological evidence (Davies, 1992, p. 24). Davies concludes that this process has clouded the sight of the real biblical and historical Israel:

> Exporting a literary construct and dumping it into Iron Age Palestine has succeeded in creating a 'history of ancient Israel'. But it has also interfered with the real history of Palestine . . . For . . . there *was* a population of Iron Age Palestine, including a kingdom called Israel . . . (Davies, 1992, p. 31)

The crux of the problem is what constitutes real history. The mistake is to read a literary account of the past as though it were a documentary, scientifically tested, record of events.

Looking seriously at the text

The historical roots of Israel remain to be explored by the tool of biblical archaeology which itself needs refining (for more on this see Chapter 5). What then is to be said of the book of Joshua's account of conquest? Working from within the text itself, one can point to the theme of conquest as an important symbol in this book. Whoever the audience of the text was, the author was keen to emphasize the validity of a religious tradition which came from outside the country. Although this was an alien culture, it was authorized to control society since its deity, the Lord of Israel, controlled the territory concerned and was giving the aliens the right of political power there. Taking Davies's view that Joshua (among other books) is shaped by the needs of a group of people returning to Judah from deportation to other parts of the Babylonian/Persian territories, it would be possible to argue that such an attitude could be used to bolster up a minority elite which was struggling to find acceptance among a resident population which viewed them as inauthentic foreigners.

Investigating further the theme of conquest leads the reader to notice how the text stresses the need to be Israelite and how outsiders are excluded from a role in the national system. But then Rahab, an outsider and a woman, is allowed a place in Israel (Josh 2; 6:17), whereas Achan, an insider, is unworthy of life in Israel since he brings disaster on his people by retaining booty which had been banned by divine command (Josh 7). There are clear indications in this material that a deliberate attempt has been made to organize sections of material into an overall message which draws its power from the way in which contrasting stories are brought into balance with each other. The narrative has been carefully crafted to carry theological and cultural ideas, thus forming a sophisticated literary genre which has a life of its own separate from the events which lie behind it. Holding all together is the constant editing of Deuteronomistic thought, expressed through the actions and speeches of the Lord of Israel, and in the phrase 'And the Lord said to Joshua', for instance, which is used repeatedly in chapters 3–6 to move the story on.

A recent monograph by K. L. Younger (1990) takes seriously the nature of Joshua 1–11 as a conquest narrative. Younger reminds the reader that *all* historical works are shaped by the presuppositions of the author. It is the historian who gathers evidence for a work and then puts individual elements into a coherent framework of chronology, of cause and effect, which gives each unit fresh meaning. The historian has a goal in mind, an idea or arguement to express – and this is true of all historians, ancient and modern.

The ancient writers of Conquest Accounts had a style of their own, suggests Younger. By an in-depth examination of surviving Assyrian, Hittite and Egyptian conquest stories Younger identifies key literary tools of this genre. These can then be compared with the Joshua text. Such a comparison reveals that Joshua 1–11 is another example of a literary genre of the ancient Near East. Themes such as the occupation of a whole region and the linking of the group as a whole to one man, Joshua, and all Israel with him, are revealed as literary tools used in this style of text to stress the successful control of events, usually by a great king.

The social function of these texts is imperialistic, they justify the rule and authority of an imperial state and its autocratic ruler. This raises again the subject of the purpose of the Deuteronomistic texts, as this is viewed by the modern reader. Whitelam argues that before the real nature of the text as historical evidence can be evaluated, the reader must examine the manner in which later ages have imparted meaning by reading in their own 'imperialist' perspectives in order to endorse their own modern cultures. The task is to return the historical origins of Israel to its native culture, Palestine. Younger's work offers the viewpoint that imperialist intent is not simply a function of modern society but was operative also in the ancient world.

Whitelam comes to his conclusions partly through the influence of recent archaeological research on the material remains of historical cultures. Younger comes to his under the influence of surviving comparative literature from the ancient Near East. This variety of approach reminds the reader that the process of situating the relatively small literary collection in the OT in the context of scattered and fragmentary evidence which has survived from the vast area and timespan usually called the ancient Near East is not a task which leads to consensus among scholars. Just as the modern world is experienced by its citizens as complex and multi-layered in meaning, so too the ancient world must have been to the people of its day. How would they have evaluated the story of the book of Joshua? What would the Syro-Palestinians of the Late Bronze Age have made of its message? That of course is the critical issue. *All* accounts offered by contemporary scholarship are modern ones, since the people of the past canot be interrogated directly by modern interviewers . . . 'Now, did Jericho really collapse like that? You were there weren't you? What did you see? . . .'

The matter of the historical origins of Israel in Palestine is then in process of discernment – it awaits further comment and further evidence from the soil of Syro-Palestine. All commentators agree

that there was a redistribution of population and the growth of
new social forms in the central highlands of Palestine at the turn
of the Bronze Ages. But how far the book of Joshua is an accurate
picture of those events is highly debated.

3

Judges and the society of ancient Israel

Whereas Joshua focuses on the acquisition of land through conquest, thus providing a basis for Israelite society in Palestine, Judges explores the kind of life lived by Israel as it establishes itself in the Land. There is further material concerning the division of landholding among the tribes, together with stories which relate how different territories were held by Israelites despite many threats to their control from opposing groups. In this book, as in Joshua, Israel is viewed as a separate entity, a selfcontained society set apart from surrounding cultures. Once again the focus of the book is on the control which the Lord of Israel had over human affairs and on his support for his chosen people.

There are, however, some interesting differences between the scene presented in Judges and that in Joshua. The overall impression given in Joshua is that of a rapid and thorough conquest of the Land; in Judges it is clear that Israel only has partial control of Palestine and that a number of other societies share that territory. Chapter 1 of the book details the areas of land which each tribe should have acquired and remarks that in a number of instances the tribe concerned failed to win territory (e.g. Judg 1:29). Modern scholars such as Mayes (1985) have argued that these are two parallel versions of how the Land was gained and have suggested that the approach of Judges is more satisfactory than that of Joshua as an explanation of what actually happened. Archaeological evidence, discussed in the last chapter, gives no support to the idea that a violent, total invasion of Palestine was carried out in the relevant time period. It seems more likely that any movement of peoples into Palestine took place gradually over a considerable number of years.

The History of the tribes

In chapter 2, verse 10 the text of Judges records the end of the initial settlement of the Land. Verse 11 moves on to the history of the tribes in the Land. It has already become clear, in Judges, that Israel is one people among others which are dwelling in the Land. The book now records what happened to Israel in this context. However, from the beginning there is a formalized, literary presentation of events. Verses 11–23 of Chapter 2 give an overview of the typical nature of events, and paint a picture which gives a particular theological slant to history. Israel has left other groups with their deities in the Land, so now, left to their own devices the Israelites go after the Baals, the gods of other nations, and neglect to worship their own patron deity. As a result they drift away from God and God in turn abandons them. Other groups win military victories over Israel and their survival is threatened. Each time this happens the people cry to the God of Israel, turning to worship him in their need. Each time the Lord listens to their cry and has pity on them. He raises up a judge to be their deliverer. This period, then, is the 'days of the judges'. There is no genealogical connection between these leaders, rather they are individuals empowered by God in their time of need, whose rule ends when the emergency is over.

The following chapters of Judges detail the rise and achievements of a number of these charismatic figures, each person having their own separate narrative in the collection of stories. Their role as judges is more that of military might than an institutional function of setting up a legal system and hearing cases, although there are hints of that role in the story of Deborah. The story of Gideon (Judg 6–8) raises the wider issue of rule over all Israel when the people ask Gideon to set up a dynastic system of inherited power (Judg 8:22). This is followed by the account of Abimelech's attempt to be king over Israel – an attempt which failed (Judg 9). Israel then returns to a system of judges, recorded quite simply in a list of names of judges in chapter 12. Finally the story of Samson is told at some length.

Judges and leaders

But what is the historical value of this structuring of Israel's past? It is possible that the book of Judges contains traces of memory of tales told about great heroes of the past, but the way in which Samson's story is told, which is similar to the style of a modern historical novel, serves to alert the reader to the probable gap between the narrative as it now exists and the original events. It becomes difficult to draw the line between events remembered somewhat hazily and invention of events. As the text stands, it does not give the reader a full report on the social and political structure of Israel at this time, but focuses on the theme of warfare and conquest.

Each of the deliverers is renowned for feats of military success against the peoples of the Land. Thus the women who are singled out for notice in this male environment are those who abet or perform deeds of physical strength such as Deborah in her urging of warfare on Barak, and Jael who crushes Sisera's head with a tent peg (Judg 4). The story of Samson focuses on supernatural physical power and on its loss. Samson is destined to be a deliverer (Judg 13), but the women he associates with are prevailed upon to find out the source of his power so that Israel's enemies can deprive him of it. Samson finally admits to Delilah that his power lies in his uncut hair. At the climax of the story Samson kills his enemies by sacrificing his own life, pulling down the house on all their heads (Judg 16).This is the story of a great folk hero and his charismatic power, but it is not an account of a formally organized state and its institutions.

Israel's social structures

One of the major issues that the nature of these accounts raises is that of the social structure of Israel at this time. How exactly was Israel organized? The OT presents Israel as emerging from Egypt as a nation. The conquest narratives in Joshua assume that there existed a centrally organized society which had a single leader, Joshua, and which was the same reality as the Israelite army. But there are few other details about the civil institutions of Israel. Instead Israel, in Judges, is family-based and relies on the individual heads of kin groups for security. The times of weakness call forth a single leader but, essentially, that deliverer depends on his immediate neighbours for support, forming them into a temporary warband.

Israel appears to be a federation of related social units, the largest of which is the tribe, then comes the clan or kin group. The smallest unit is that of the household or family (the father's house). This picture of Israel is presented in Joshua 7 where Joshua is seeking one Israelite who has broken a divine command. Joshua brings the people to the test first by tribes, then by families and then by households, until the actual sinner is identified.

Israel appears to be a society composed of individual units, the tribes, which may be brought together from time to time. From the biblical account it seems that there was a fixed number of tribes, who all took their origin from one ancestor, Jacob. Joshua, for instance, neatly refers to the division of land between twelve equal groups. It should be noted, however, that the OT does not always give the same details about these units. On the one hand the tribe of Levi is included in the twelve and Joseph is a single tribe (as in Gen 29–30) and on the other Levi is left out and Joseph split into two tribes – Manasseh and Ephraim (as in Num 26).

It is likely that twelve named tribes was part of the later stages of the editing of this material. But this leaves open the possibility that Israel was, in general, a tribal society. Modern scholars have taken an interest in this social history of early Israel and have given various accounts of how it all worked. One of the issues they have addressed is the extent to which it is reasonable to argue that Israel, at this stage, was a single society, even if made up of independent social groupings. Was the All-Israel picture of the overall editor of the Deuteronomistic Histories historically correct? One of the major scholars who would argue for the historicity of All-Israel is M. Noth.

Martin Noth and Israel's history

M. Noth, in his *History of Israel*, describes the Israelites as migratory peoples who came to settle in the highlands of Canaan. Their migration was part of a general movement of peoples at the end of the Bronze Age:

> This great movement, of which the settlement of the Israelite tribes was part and which consisted of many different elements, took place during the transition from the Bronze to the Iron Age, proceeding from the Syrian-Arabian desert into the bordering agricultural lands. (Noth, 1960, p. 83)

After each tribe had settled in its locality within Palestine there existed a federation of All-Israel. The common aspect of this federation was its adherence to a particular deity, the Lord of Israel. Noth argued that this created a special form of social organization which he described as a sacral association of tribes, an 'ancient Israelite amphictyony' (Noth, 1960, p. 88).

In using the term 'amphictyony' (a term taken directly from Ancient Greek society), Noth was comparing Israel with other local federations of peoples known about from the ancient world, such as those of ancient Greece. In these comparative organizations a bond was created by a common cult. Members met for particular festivals at the central shrine whose upkeep was the responsibility of the member groups. This approach utilizes both the concept of smaller sub-units in society and the belief that there was a broader understanding of social identity than simply local ties.

Noth argued that this model could be used to explain the history of ancient Israel. He pointed to texts which refer to central places of worship, in the Deuteronomistic Histories, places where the Ark of the Lord was maintained and to which Israel came to worship its God. Joshua 24, for instance, tells of Joshua bringing all the tribes together at Shechem. Noth argued that there must have been a series of institutions connected with Israelite worship which held society together. The OT, however, does not contain any details of these structures. What it does include are references to a common law which forms the Covenant between God and his people and which is remembered at common gatherings at a central shrine.

The historian, said Noth, should focus on the theme of Law as provider of a centralizing force which drew the tribal groups together for cultic gatherings. These gatherings concentrated less on sacrifice than on

> . . . blessings and curses for the observance and infringement of the statutes of the law, and the foundation of the validity of these statutes was the covenant between God and people which according to Jos. xxiv, 25 was regularly reviewed at the central shrine. (Noth, 1960, p. 100)

Thus, according to Noth, Israel's identity was shaped by communal gatherings in the name of a common deity, but this assembly was coloured by the concept of a contract or covenant between God and people as a result of which certain social rules were binding on the people:

> Israel's speciality did not consist in a particular and unique form of worship at the central shrine but in the fact that it was subject to a divine law which was recited at the tribal gatherings at regular intervals. (Noth, 1960, p. 101)

The story of Moses and the deliverance from Egypt functioned as part of the sacred traditions connected with these tribal gatherings.

In the years which have followed Noth's publications it has become clear that his picture of the past is too clearcut and relies too literally on the details of the narratives in the Deuteronomistic Histories. The clarity of the All-Israel perspective has, for instance, been challenged since close reading of the text reveals that each hero (heroine) is originally a separate local figure and that the impression of unity is largely created by the editing of these stories together. That is, it is part of the later stages of the tradition about Israel's past. Scholars have also argued that it is not viable to compare Palestine in the eleventh century BCE with Greece in the sixth century BCE. The amphictyonic theory is, therefore, now generally discarded. But that does not mean that it is incorrect to describe Israel as a tribal society.

The Tribes of YHWH

N. Gottwald is another scholar who has attempted to give a social history of early Israel (Gottwald, 1979). He focused his account of ancient Israel's social system on the central concept of 'tribe' as a system of social organization. The focus of this organization is the term 'tribe', which functions as the equivalent of house or people. Tribe is then broken down to subsections such as household or 'House of the Father', also described by commentators on the text as 'Families'. Three levels of society are ultimately delineated, using the OT books – namely, tribe, clan or kin and family or household. The manner of organization works from the bottom, the smallest unit of family up to the largest unit of tribe. Israelites were first of all members of extended families which came together for security and common goals, as necessity dictated. There was, for Gottwald, an essential egalitarianism in Israel's social systems. People chose to ally with each other rather than having a hierarchical political system imposed on them from above, as in a city-state culture.

Gottwald argued that this new form of social organization emerged in opposition to the hierarchical and elitist city cultures of Palestine. There was a form of peasant revolt which produced the tribal system linked to an agricultural style of living:

> Our basic approach . . . has been to make a synchronic typological crosscut of the sociopolitical structure of Amarna Canaan, in which we have noted a persistent . . . movement towards increasing disin-

tegration of the . . . feudal-Imperial interlock, a movement which has as its terminal horizon the emergence of early Israel as the antithesis of the . . . Canaanite system. (Gottwald, 1979, p. 489)

Israel was fused together from various social components such as discontented agriculturalists, Apiru bands, refugees from Egypt and other social 'outlaws' of Late Bronze Age Canaan.

But what made Israel stable and unique, and facilitated its takeover of power in the area was its religious faith. Religious ideology made a harmonious whole with social and political systems and so created a new culture, that of 'mono-Yahwism'. Israelite society developed from Israelite religion. Gottwald proposed 'that mono-Yahwism was the function of sociopolitical organisation in pre-monarchic Israel' (Gottwald, 1979, p. 611). He argued that 'mono-Yahwism . . . was . . . of critical significance as an axial form-giving, and energy-releasing reality in literary and intellectual culture, in economics, in social organisation, in military affairs and in self-government' (Gottwald, 1979, p. 616).

In his version of Israelite society Gottwald thus combined the insights of social-scientific methods with evidence drawn from the OT. In general this has paved the way for later scholars by encouraging an interplay of modern sociological and anthropological methodologies with biblical exegesis. But Gottwald's theory of mono-Yahwism has itself been criticized and supplanted:

Finally, scholars in general have rejected the 'peasants' revolt' model because it is too obviously a projection of modern marxist notions of 'class-conflict' onto Ancient Israel [and] . . . it invokes as the 'engine' that drives social change an idealistic concept of 'Yahwism' that lacks any external corroboration. (Dever, 1997, p. 25)

Basic issues

None of these theories has succeeded in winning support from scholarship. Yet the basic elements of them are agreed by all, namely, that it is likely that 'tribal' is a good adjective to use about early Israel and that this form of society came about because of the shift in population patterns in Palestine in the Late Bronze Age. Archaeology has provided a reasonably clear image of Palestine at this date. The focus of population in the Late Bronze Ages was the city states of the coastal plains, whose rulers owed loyalty to the Egyptian rulers since Egypt was the dominant power in the region. Movement of Sea Peoples (Phoenicians) had led to invasion from the coast itself and, although Egypt had defeated these foreign intrusions they had allowed the formation of a five-city settlement of Sea Peoples in the costal strip by Gaza. The members of this culture now became known as Philistines.

Towards the end of the Late Bronze Age the region became destabilized. This was partly because there was a crisis of power in Egypt which weakened its control of Palestine, leaving local kings to vie with each other. Since one city state was the same as another and the concept of nationalism was not involved, discontented inhabitants moved from one city to the next providing a floating, migrant people who might live on the fringes of cultivated areas for some time and prey on city-dwellers. In addition it may be that the Philistine league saw its chance to expand its control inland. All these changes led to the decline of city culture, with more people dwelling permanently in the poorer agricultural area of the central highlands. It is this shift which eventually gave rise to Israel:

> ... if we follow the line demarcated by the Amarna Letters, the inscription from Beth-Shan, and the Merneptah inscription, and compare this with information contained in the OT ... we may see the outline of an alternative society which emerged in the mountainous region of Palestine in the second half of the Late Bronze Age and the beginning of the Iron Age. (Lemche, 1988, p. 89)

The development of archaeology in Israel has added to our knowledge of this process. In the early stages of the discipline excavators were interested in the remains of the large and famous cities of the Near East and little evidence about rural areas was available to the biblical scholar. I. Finkelstein has remedied this gap with his series of village excavations in the central highlands of Palestine:

> Particularly in the mountain areas, but also in the various plains and in the Negev, numerous newly-established villages have been identified which were situated outside the area of the former city-states and only in exceptional cases exceeded a half to one hectare ... in area. (Fritz, 1995, p. 13)

V. Fritz's work *The City in Ancient Israel* (1995) gives an account of urban and village sites from the Bronze Ages through to the Iron Ages, using evidence drawn from the many excavations carried out since 1948 in Israel. This research gives a new foundation for examining biblical narrative since it provides the picture of actual habitation in the area, drawn from its material remains. But lack of written material which would cross-reference with written texts from the OT makes it impossible to bring the archaeological results directly to bear on the stories in the book of Judges.

Reconstructions

It seems likely that 'tribal' is a reasonable way of describing Israelite society but exactly how this tribal system functioned is hard to pin down. An attempt to describe household existence has recently been made by C. Meyers in her article on 'The family in early Israel' (in Perdue *et al.* (eds), 1997, pp. 1–47). For her study Meyers draws on Joshua, Judges and some Pentateuchal passages as well as archaeological evidence and some comparative aspects of cultural anthropology. Meyers starts with the geographical features of the highlands since environment often defines what can take place within it. The highlands setting shaped habitation and cultivation patterns – small villages and subsistence farming, for instance, are the result of poor terrain and scanty water supplies. From this basis Meyers constructs a picture of the typical activities of a highland village and its households, reflecting on gender specific roles, for instance:

> The experience of senior males with respect to the nuances of soil terrain, climate, tool types, crop choices, and livestock management was gradually passed to the next generation as older male children were apprenticed to the fathers, uncles and grandfathers of the compound family . . . A similar pattern of transmitting knowledge across generations affected female lives. In their daily activities, older females passed on to younger ones all the technical aspects of gardening, food processing, meal preparation, textile production, and other tasks within their specialised economic domains. (Meyers, 1997, p. 30)

Other scholars have turned more fully to comparative anthropology for models with which to explain the picture given in Judges. A. Malamat and N. Lohfink (cited by D. Fiensy, 'Using the Nuer culture of Africa', in Chalcroft (ed.) 1997) have re-used the concept of 'segmentary society' as found among African tribal structures such as that of the Nuer. In this social system members belong to clans within tribes. There is no central authority and membership is created through genealogical ties. In a crisis power can be given to a single individual whose authority lasts only during that emergency. Individuals 'know their place' in this kind of society despite its lack of formal, central institutions and have a common sense of belonging.

There is a good deal of similarity between this African tribal system and the evidence for early Israel to be found in the book of Judges. The African evidence is that a society can exist as an independent grouping with such a structure and is not unstable or lacking in permanence. This model may be the nearest scholarship can get to the historical reality of the Late Bronze/early Iron Age Israel, at the present.

The continuity of tribalism

One further point needs to be made here, concerning the interpretation of the Deuteronomistic Histories and their picture of agricultural tribalism. The history of the region shows that the collapse of cities and the rise of early Israel was not a unique phenomenon in terms of the balance between urban and rural lifestyles seeming to be in flux. Fritz (1995) shows that there were in fact city cultures in the Early Bronze Age which collapsed for no reason that historians can now trace. The failure of these cities led to a period of small village settlements before a second wave of city culture in the Middle Bronze Age II. It was this phase whose decline saw the rise of Israel. Israel itself became a city culture, according to the biblical text.

After the fall of Jersualem in the sixth century BCE Judah became a small province in a foreign empire and may have suffered economic decline. It may have been partly for these reasons that the Persian rulers decided on a programme of local renewal, focusing around a newly-constructed Temple state in Jerusalem, which operated within the general structures of family and kinship systems. There is an emphasis, for instance, on marriage of priests within Israelite kinship groups and the setting aside of foreign wives (e.g. Ezra 9).

All of this evidence indicates that family-based society was a common form of life in Palestine. It could well be that while the general picture of Israel's origins as tribal is sound, some of the details of the book of Judges, such as that of twelve named tribes, for instance, owe more to the form of tribalism operating in the fifth-century province of Judah than to the past society of the eleventh century BCE.

Summary

The two books of Joshua and Judges appear to provide the reader with information about the early life of Israel: Joshua with a history of settlement and Judges with the early social history of Israel. Scholars have agreed that this material should be seriously considered, but the somewhat literal reading of the text by the first generations of modern biblical researchers have more recently come under criticism. The growth of biblical archaeology is generally seen to be the means of moving forward on the question of Israel's origins, but the material remains of civilizations cannot provide a complete picture of life in an area. In particular, with Israel there is a considerable gap between the sophisticated literary texts of the OT and the mainly non-written traces of habitation in Bronze Age Palestine.

With regard to the manner in which Israel emerged, there is less support nowadays for the conquest view even though that conflicts with the biblical story. It can be argued that population movements were more gradual and varied than Joshua depicts while at the same time allowing for some immigration of peoples from Egypt. However, the main focus of scholarship is on the internal nature of the growth of Israel. Here the book of Judges provides the reader with the concept of tribe and family. But the details of actual tribal groups and their heroic members cannot be supported from non-biblical evidence.

4

1 and 2 Samuel: social and political leadership

The description of early Israel as a society with a localized and kinship-based structure raises the question of when and how Israel arrived at the structures of a state system – that is, at a social system which has a permanent and centralized leadership supported by a public administration. In the OT the term 'kingdom' is usually taken by modern scholarship to refer to a state system incorporating a nation. In the Deuteronomistic Histories the books of Kings imply the existence of an Israelite and of a Judaean state, each based on city culture, with state officials, standing army and, above all, a king. So the question can be asked: At what point did this social system emerge and how did it develop?

Textually, the answer to this is to be found in the two books of Samuel where kingship develops through the careers of two men, Saul and David. By the end of his reign David has acquired control over large parts of Syro-Palestine, establishing his capital city at Jerusalem. This can be contrasted with the situation early on in 1 Samuel in which Israel is in disarray following the loss of the Ark of the Lord to the Philistines (1 Sam 6–8). Once again the biblical narrative can be investigated via archaeological evidence so that its message can be checked out for historicity.

From tribes to kingdom

The picture given by the Deuteronomistic Histories is of a rapid rise of statehood. The lives of two men serve to move Israel from tribal society to kingdom. Israel appears, in fact, already to have been neatly structured into tribes with a common identity and only needed actual kings to confirm this centralized focus of All-Israel, moving from federation to single state. However, it has been pointed out in previous chapters that the image of Israel as a tightly shaped social grouping in the Late Bronze Age is heavily criticized by biblical scholars. This makes the biblical picture of the rise of kingship seem even more extraordinary in its speed and success, and therefore even less likely to convince the reader that the narrative conveys an accurate picture of real life historical change. Social systems rely upon economic and population growth; usually shifts in size of population and wealth occur gradually over a long period of time.

The Deuteronomistic picture of events can be quickly summarized. The focus is on the rise of kingship as an institution. The first signs of this type of leadership are to be found in the book of Judges, in the careers of Gideon and Abimelech. Both men have the chance to take up an institutionalized leadership role; Gideon holds back (Judg 8) but Abimelech seizes his opportunity. The result, however, is disastrous (Judg 9). Abimelech murders his rivals, thus bringing blood guilt on his own head, and dies in a minor skirmish while besieging Thebez (Judg 9:53–55). Kingship is in abeyance after that until the two books of Samuel which describe the careers of Saul and David, both of them connected with the theme of kingship.

With Saul (1 Sam) the history of kings proper begins and by the time of David the institution is fully established (2 Sam). David is recognized ruler by All-Israel (2 Sam 5) and creates a central focus for his kingdom in the city of Jerusalem, the site of his own palace and of God's dwelling-place (2 Sam 6). Although David does not construct a stone house for God, he does bring the Ark of the Lord to rest permanently in Jerusalem. The combination of secular and religious powers signals the creation of a new form of political organization which is to be permanent, expressed through the symbolic phrase 'house of David'. In 2 Sam 7 God promises to care for David's son and to make him heir, together with his sons after him, provided that these generations of kings remain loyal to the national deity who is their 'father'.

Davidic empire and archaeology

The impression created by this narrative outlined above is that David became a great and famous ruler. The man who, by personal energy (together with divine support) brought together individual tribes, led them against the Philistines and other opponents and so carved out a large territory in Palestine which could be labelled the kingdom of Israel. Stories such as the defeat of Goliath by the simple shepherd boy, David, leave the reader with the picture of a charismatic hero. Saul killed thousands of the enemy, the women sing, but David slaughtered tens of thousands (1 Sam 18:7). It seems fair to describe such a great war-leader as the head of an empire. By 'empire' modern readers understand the bringing under one ruler of large areas of land once separately governed. This may include groups with different languages and customs as well as separate political systems. The term indicates a high degree of military power and back up structures to support military conquest. In ancient Palestine such a title is given to the rule by Egypt in the Bronze Age and to the Assyrian and Babylonian powers in the Iron Age.

Great rulers of large empires tend to leave behind some traces of their power, traces which archaeologists can then investigate. Thus information can be collected from Nineveh concerning Babylonian power, including the library of the rulers. Tribute pillars have been found which point to Assyrian control in northern Palestine; the Amarna letters point to Egyptian control in an earlier period. But there is a great silence with regard to David and Solomon. The excavated ruins of habitation in Iron Age Syro-Palestine have so far yielded no major signs of Davidic influence – no victory inscriptions, no remains of palaces which can securely be related to David. It may be argued that part of the problem is that Jersualem, David's capital city, cannot be properly excavated because of its modern religious associations with three world religions, Judaism, Christianity, Islam. But that ought not to account for silence elsewhere in the region.

Recently one piece of evidence has emerged from the ruins. Excavations at Tell-Dan have brought to light an inscription which appears to relate to the 'house of David'. This inscription records the victories of an invading king, including, possibly, success over the house of David. There are some problems about this evidence. The stone surface is weathered and the wording fragmentary. A fierce debate has ensued among biblical scholars as to the weight of the evidence. It is hard to decipher the inscription, so is it certain that the reference is indeed to the house of David? Secondly, even if the text does make such a reference it is a passing one. It may indicate that David was a ruler whose dynasty governed in the region, but it does not prove the historicity of the entire David narrative. David's story is told in 1 and 2 Samuel in a series of short stories. There is David's unhappy relationship with Saul (1 Sam 18–30) and his abuse of power in committing adultery with Bathsheba (2 Sam 11–12). These narratives are told in a sophisticated manner (see Part two of this book) and are not rough chronicles of public royal events. The details of these stories have not yet been authenticated as events of the tenth century BCE.

The argument from silence

Scholars have responded in opposing ways to the lack of material corroboration of the biblical stories from archaeological research. K. Whitelam, on the one hand, has argued that there is no reality to the Davidic state imaged in 1 and 2 Samuel. Essentially, he suggests, the lack of concrete archaeological evidence for Davidic power, such as inscriptions and large public monuments, together with the generally low level of economic development in tenth-century BCE Palestine, supports the view that there was no Davidic empire. He contrasts his conclusions with those of other scholars who have written modern historiographical accounts of David. Whereas he is dubious about the figure of David, others emphasize his central importance in the expansion of Israel:

> It is not simply the assumption that the rise of an Israelite state, and in particular the Davidic monarchy, brings us to history proper but that this is the defining moment of Israelite history and so of the region as a whole. (Whitelam, 1996, p. 128)

In those treatments of David which emphasize his key role in Israelite development, the rise of the Israelite state is connected to a 'Great Men of History' theory. In this approach powerful human leaders themselves shape society and and are foundations for innovation and change. The emphasis here is on David's function in providing a 'personal union' of individual tribes in Israel. Whitelam argues that these opinions stem from the context of the historiographers themselves. In using the term 'historiographers' Whitelam is making a serious distinction between what actually happened in the past (history) and written accounts of past events (historiography). The current debates about the validity of Israeli expansionism in the West Bank are the setting for the presentation of a great leader of the past who laid claim successfully to these same land areas (Whitelam, 1996, p. 147).

Other scholars wish to accept the biblical account as containing some traces of historical events; Schafer-Lichtenberger (1966), for instance, believes that it is a question of how one interprets the idea of state. It may well be inaccurate to compare Davidic Israel with the great Egyptian and Mesopotamian empires of the ancient

Near East but that does not mean that it is wholly wrong to label it a state. She argues that it is unlikely that evidence would be found for a small state, except in the records of a greater local power. Since the tenth century appears to have been a time when both Egyptian and Mesopotamian nations suffered a decline in power and so temporarily lost control of Palestine, it is not probable that Israel's political actions were recorded. Thus there are no tribute pillars from this period and so no external references to Israel as a vassal state.

Schafer-Lichtenberger goes on to offer a possible understanding of a small state in these conditions. She remarks that modern readers interpret the word 'state' through their modern social experience of a large public sector administration and economy. However there are alternative interpretations available here. One possibility is the patrimonial state (Schafer-Lichtenberger, 1996, p. 83) in which there is a centralized control functioning through an extended household system. Public officials are members of the royal household and owe allegiance to the ruler who is himself part of a narrow band of elite families, thus control is exercised outside the royal household through royal estates. This is still a state system, although it is not the same as the modern industrial state. It could be that this is the kind of state which is indicated in biblical texts concerning the kingship of Saul and David.

Whereas Whitelam was concerned to highlight what he thought to be inauthentic assumptions about the past and its political structures, Schafer-Lichtenberger passes from a quick condemnation of inauthentic modern imaging of the past to offer an alternative model for exploring the reigns of Saul and David as portrayed in the OT. Whitelam's approach tends to cast continuing doubt on the reliability of the stories in 1 and 2 Samuel, Schafer–Lichtenberger's view, by contrast, is that some reliability can be posited for these texts. Whitelam focuses on 'empire' which he dismantles as a usable term, while Schafer-Lichtenberger endorses the value of the term 'state'.

Leadership models

Underlying the debate concerning the historicity or otherwise of the Deuteronomistic account of Saul and David are issues concerning the terminology which modern commentators use and how these terms relate to the vocabulary of the original literature. As indicated above, some of the debates concern labels for political organisation – state, empire, kingdom . . . Other debates centre around the terms for leaders themselves – prince (*nagid*) and King (*melek*). These issues of terminology will now be examined in more detail.

The essential term for political organization in the Deuteronomistic Histories is 'kingdom', a term which focuses on the rule of one man over his territory. Although David is connected with Jerusalem, the picture of Israelite kingship is not that of the city-state cultures of the Late Bronze Age Palestine. There the king ruled over a city or town and its immediate environment. There was no special ethnic stress, one city state was as good as the next. By contrast, David and Saul are kings whose control is of the people of Israel and the geographical area inhabited by that people. Apart from Jerusalem, the Deuteronomistic texts mention no major city centres until later in the monarchy – Israel appears to be a largely village-based society, a picture which coincides with the picture of settlement derived from the archaeological record for this time and area.

But is there a place for arguing that Israel nevertheless displayed signs of developing into a single state in the tenth century BCE, using the biblical record as evidence? Returning to Schafer-Lichtenberger's article gives some basis for investigation. She defines the meaning of 'state' as an organized and monopolized political power, where leadership is the highest authority, influencing the distribution of power and the shaping of society. This model does, indeed, seem to fit within the biblical evidence on Saul and David and can be tied in with the biblical term *melek* (king). The king is thus the head of a real state system, but one based on his own inherited and acquired resources.

A good description of the biblical meaning of this term is given in 1 Samuel, where Samuel discusses with the God of Israel the people's desire for a king like those of other nations. 1 Samuel 8 implies that this king has absolute authority and a good deal of power since he accumulates his own wealth and demands services from his subjects, in his household, his fields and his wars. Such a king would also have religious and civil duties for the prosperity and success of his state, which is the feature of kingship which Israel is looking for in 1 Samuel 8:19–20: 'that our king may govern us and go out before us and fight our battles'.

The presence of a debate on the meaning and value of kingship here implies a recognition that a major shift in social and political structures was about to take place. In the text the focus is on the religious meaning of this change, that is, the abandoning of the Lord as Israel's king in exchange for a human model of government. But shorn of this setting the text remains evidence for a shift in Israelite society set in the Early Iron Age, at least in the minds of the later editors of the biblical material. This shift involves a new political term, that of king, whereas elsewhere the book of 1 Samuel uses the term *nagid* (prince) for Saul and David. The two terms appear to be interchangeable in the texts which describe the rise of monarchy, although the term king dominates in accounts of the later monarchy, such as the reign of Solomon (cf 1 Kgs 4).

The title of prince appears to involve a lesser sense of control and so is nearer to the non-dynastic leadership of Judges. It could be argued that this role is essentially military. Accounts of Saul and David are full of details of the battles fought by them. Both men have their own warriors drawn from close kinship circles and can draw upon men from other tribes, as in 1 Samuel 11 where the Ammonite victory over Jabesh-Gilead leads to Saul's seizure of military control of the situation, whereby he sends out a sign to all Israel in a portion of slaughtered cattle. As a result he musters all Israel to fight the enemy. The root of the title prince could be that of such military functions, an idea floated by Flanagan in his article on 'Chiefs in Israel' (in Chalcroft (ed.), pp. 142–67).

Flanagan argues that both Saul and David were chiefs and that that fits them into a pattern of development of social structures recognized by cultural anthropologists – that is, band, tribe, chiefdom, kingship (state). Saul and David had a chief's role and their careers represent the intermediate stage between tribe and statehood: an argument which lessens the gap between biblical text and modern knowledge about political development generally (as referred to earlier in this chapter). According to Flanagan (1997, p. 147), a chief's authority is normally vested in skills of warfare, dancing, solidifying alliances and redistributing goods. Flanagan argues that both Saul and David's careers in 1 and 2 Samuel show elements of chiefdom and chiefly rule.

Flanagan's arguments would give weight to the biblical text as reflector of authentic evidence about tenth-century BCE Israel, but how far can this be taken? There is a general similarity between the conditions described in 1 and 2 Samuel and sociological models drawn from comparative anthropological research. It seems logical to suggest that both Saul and David could have been single leaders like the judges, and that what changed was the establishment of the house of Saul and the house of David – allowing their kinship groups continued authority to control Israel even in peace. As to the causes of this change, there are Flanagan's suggestions of social and economic shifts in the area, reflected in political change. It has to be noted, though, that there is practically no evidence for specifically Israelite economic conditions from the archaeological record of this period. There is also the possibility that with the collapse of Egyptian hegemony, Palestine was 'up for grabs'. Military pressure on Israel from her neighbours, especially the Philistine league, meant a near continuous need for a central warleader.

But that does not underwrite the authenticity of the details of Saul's and David's careers. D. Edelman (in Fritz and Davies (eds), 1996, pp. 142–60) has examined 'Saul ben Kish in history and tradition'. She suggests that it is possible to make some distinctions. Certain motifs in the story come from the literary nature of the text, items such as: the good and evil spirits in Saul (1 Sam 11/1 Sam 16:14), the friendship of David and Jonathan (1 Sam 20), Saul's death scene (1 Sam 31). On the other hand the details of battles fought and won may have some historical value, together with the Saulide genealogy in 1 Samuel 9:1 and Saul's connections with Gibeon (Edelman, 1996, pp. 152–4). She concludes 'My own recreation posits that Saul emerged initially as a petty king of Gibeon, and expanded from that palace state to the neighbourhood' (Edelman, 1996, p. 156).

A further point which must be noted takes the reader back to the term 'Deuteronomistic'. All these separate stories are now linked together as part of the evidence for God's relationship with his people, a relationship in which innocence/sin on the people's part matches blessing/cursing by the deity. The fact that parts of 1 Samuel refer to Saul as prince only and reserve the title of king for David's establishment of a monarchy may reflect the views of the OT editors many centuries later, in the sixth to the fourth centuries BCE, when David was defined in text as the type of an ideal leader, one whose harmony with the nation's deity led to success and prosperity for the whole people (cf. Psalm 72, which gives a picture of such a leader). The effect of this is to shift a competition between rival chieftains for overall control of resources inside Israelite areas into a destined succession of leaders, each in turn chosen and endorsed by the deity.

Other forms of leadership in 1 and 2 Samuel

A form of leadership parallel to that offered by Saul and David is to be found, in 1 and 2 Samuel, in the figure of Samuel himself. Samuel figures as prophet and as seer. His story begins with a birth narrative highlighting the direct role played by God in Samuel's conception in response to a barren woman's prayer. As a boy, given up to the service of God, Samuel is called to be a messenger – something of a rarity since God's word is not often heard at this time (1 Sam 3:1). He is to be a prophet of the Lord, whose word comes to him and which becomes Samuel's word to the people. Thus he acts as a messenger of God, passing divine information and decisions on to fellow human beings, a task linked to the meaning of the term for prophet – (*Nabi*, a messenger).

In 1 Samuel 7:6 a further aspect of Samuel's work is highlighted when he acts as judge of the people. The scene reminds the reader of the book of Judges, since its presentation of Samuel is in the style of a past social order. Samuel features as the last of older style leadership, although it was not clear in Judges exactly what powers and duties the term 'judge' signified. Yet another feature of Samuel's functions as leader emerges in 1 Samuel 7:8. The people are threatened with enemy warbands and beg for divine assistance. Samuel acts here as priestly mediator by sacrificing a burnt offering to the Lord of Israel as a request for his support. God duly thunders against the Philistines who are dismayed and flee away (1 Sam 7:10–11).

Thus Samuel is revealed as prophet, judge and priest in these chapters and his task is summed up in 1 Samuel 7:15 where it is stated that Samuel judged Israel all the days of his life. His career involves a long-term responsibility for the people's welfare, then, a responsibility which he aims to pass on to his own sons – a sign of a move to dynastic leadership. But here the people intervene to demand a king. Samuel himself now features as kingmaker, since God sends him a sign to anoint Saul with oil as a sign of kingship (1 Sam 9:15–16). In a parallel story (1 Sam 10), Samuel is pictured as creating Saul king by the taking of lots, that is, by divination.

Once Saul is ruler, Samuel acts as a long-distance adviser on Israel's affairs, as in 1 Samuel 12. When God abandons Saul, it is Samuel whom he calls upon to anoint David king in his place. Samuel's career is closely linked with those of the early kings of Israel, even to the point of being called back from the grave when Saul, desperate for divine guidance with his war effort, seeks out a medium who raises the dead in order to reach divine foreknowledge (necromancer) and commands that she raise Samuel for him.

Seer and diviner

It is clear that the story of Samuel has been fitted into the overall shape of the Deuteronomistic Histories. The account of his life links judges with kings and offers a foretaste of the role of later prophets as critics of kingship. Beneath this surface level of the text Samuel visibly has several different functions in society. One major role is that of prophet and, particularly, of diviner. He casts lots, for instance, to gain divine guidance (1 Sam 10:20) and is a direct channel of divine words to his society (1 Sam 8:10).

Cultural anthropology is relevant to situating a figure like Samuel in its ancient Near Eastern background. In the area of prophecy there are many cross-cultural features which can be compared with Israelite prophecy. T. Overholt's *Cultural Anthropology and the Old Testament* (1996), explores the role of cultural comparisons in opening up new methods of reading the OT (ch. 1). He looks especially at the phenomenon of prophecy and of divination (ch. 3). Comparing and contrasting Samuel's role with those of other diviners from different cultures highlights the instances of divination activity in the books of 1 and 2 Samuel and gives deeper meaning to the description of Samuel himself as a seer.

F. Cryer's study *Divination in Ancient Israel and Its Near Eastern Environment*, (1994) also contributes to an understanding of the role of divination in ancient Israel. Having explored Mesopotamian and Egyptian examples of divination, Cryer turns to Israel. With regard to 1 and 2 Samuel, one of his findings is quite interesting, namely that Mesopotamian kings used divination to provide legitimacy for such actions as seizure of power and ascent to a contested throne (1994, p. 213). This offers an interesting parallel to the use of divination in the careers of Saul and David who are both attempting to establish their power more securely. Cryer indeed argues that the careers of both Saul and David are woven through with oracular activity. He also points to instances of divination in Samuel's work.

Cryer suggests that scenes of sacrifices, some carried out by Samuel, may be examples of Omen Sacrifice, an offering ritual which will be interpreted as signs providing divine guidance for future policy. Within 1 Samuel, then, it is possible to trace the work of religious figures who functioned as mediators of divine power. Samuel had a leadership role insofar as he acted as a channel for divine guidance on political and social matters, thus enabling projects in warfare, for instance, to be brought to a satisfactory conclusion.

Conclusions

It appears that the narratives of 1 and 2 Samuel are built around three types of leader – prince, king and prophet. The focus of these forms of leadership, however, is religious meaning rather than secular affairs in themselves. The three forms also circle round three characters, Samuel, Saul and David who in various ways exemplify these leadership roles. In the course of the telling of their stories, value-judgements are offered on secular society. In terms of religious leadership the role of the prophet is significant. That role should be situated historically, in the broad context of a range of divinatory practices operating in the ancient Near East, but cultural practices have been overlaid with a religious commentary which transforms the prophet from diviner to political advisor to secular leaders.

These are the types of comments which can be seen within the literary techniques of the books of 1 and 2 Samuel. If the separate story elements are treated in their own right, though, has the reader finally got in touch with the history of the tenth century BCE? That is a further issue which involves turning to the archaeological record. Comparing and contrasting the text and extant remains of society endorses the general picture of the development of new social forms in response to shifts in the political balance in Syro-Palestine in this period, but without proving the accuracy of the details of the biblical stories.

5

1 and 2 Kings and biblical archaeology

The previous chapter examined the issue of the 'rise of the monarchy' under Saul and David. It became clear that the evidence for a state of Israel in tenth-century BCE Palestine is ambiguous and conflicting. The biblical account in the books of Samuel seems to suggest that there was a quick transition from tribal federation to nation state, whereas the archaeological evidence for a Davidic empire is slight.

If any of the early kings of Israel and Judah can be associated with the concept of a state composed of Israelites, it is more likely to be Solomon than Saul or David. This raises the possibility that Solomon, consolidating his father's kingdom, created a state of some regional importance. The biblical account supports such a thesis.

Biblical Solomon

The story of Solomon is recounted in 1 Kings 1–11, which deals with his life from his accession to the throne, through a successful reign to a final decline. Solomon is portrayed as someone whose mother is ambitious for him and who paves the way for his succession to his father, David's, power. Since he is one among a number of David's children, his rise to power involves rivalry with Adonijah, who is outwitted and ultimately killed, in order to ensure Solomon's own success (1 Kgs 1–2).

By chapter 3 Solomon is described as God's chosen king, greatly in divine favour. The story of Solomon's prayer and dream focus on his excellent intelligence and discernment in judgement – a skill illustrated in the story of the two prostitutes quarrelling over the same child. This theme of a wise king climaxes in the visit of the Queen of Sheba (1 Kgs 10:1–13). Indeed Solomon stands in later tradition as a great wisdom figure, in texts such as the Wisdom of Solomon, for instance.

Wisdom was balanced with might, according to the biblical account. Chapter 4 describes the king as having high officials (verses 2–6) and regional administrators (verses 7–19). It also details the amount of provisions which the royal court could command (verses 22–24), indicating the personal wealth and control of the ruler over his land, a feature borne out by verse 25:

> And Judah and Israel dwelt in safety, from Dan even to Beer-sheba, every man under his vine and under his fig tree, all the days of Solomon.

The motif of fig and vine stresses the peaceful prosperity of the time, since these are symbols of an easy agricultural life, without the hard labour involved in producing grain crops. Finally Solomon has his standing army, composed of chariots and horsemen, the most powerful style of army at that time. The focus of this tale of power and wealth is the building of the Temple which is recorded in chapters 5–7. In chapter 8, at the climax of the story, Solomon himself acts out a priestly role by standing in the middle between people and their God and asking for blessing.

Solomon in history

But how far is this an authentic account? Just as with the story of David, it can be noted that there is no extant archaeological evidence for Solomon in terms of building inscriptions or victory records. It is also true of Solomon, of course, that the most likely place to find evidence would be in Jerusalem, where it is so difficult to excavate freely. However, a more general application of archaeological evidence can be made in order to throw light on the possible tenth-century kingdom of Solomon. D. W. Jamieson-Drake in *Scribes and Schools in Monarchic Judah* (1991), has made a thorough study of the overall archaeological data for tenth- to eighth-century BCE Judah. If the biblical record is accurate then a centralized, effective administrative system would have existed, the foundations for which would lie in basic skills of literacy among the population. Jamieson-Drake works from that perspective to wider comments on the society of the period.

For literacy in turn depends on a degree of urbanization in a society and on a developing economy. So one way into the subject is to examine evidence for settlement patterns, public works and luxury items. Increasing population, the construction of urban centres with public buildings such as fortress, palace and temple, the increasing use of luxury items (including any artefact needing a skilled craftsman and evidence of writing skills, as well as the presence of imported goods) all point to a developing culture able to support a system of reading and writing.

Allowing for various gaps in present archaeological knowledge and for the difficulty of interpreting some archaeological evidence, Jamieson-Drake concludes that there is very little evidence to support the view that the tenth century witnessed a centralized national state under Solomon capable of supporting a generally literate population, not only at the centre in Jerusalem, but also in localities within the state. The evidence points to the emergence of something approaching such a state in the eighth century BCE:

> the model which places the achievement of full statehood for Judah in the eighth century allows time for the transition from chiefdom to statehood to occur ... the institutions established by Solomon evolved and developed over time into a fullblown state by the eighth century ... (Jamieson-Drake, 1991, p. 144)

Thus it appears that Solomon as presented in the Deuteronomistic account of him is a rather larger-than-life figure, one to whom the fullness of kingly power can be attributed, as noted by V. Fritz in his article 'Monarchy and re-urbanisation: a new look at Solomon's kingdom' (Fritz, 1996), where he states:

> The king has become, as it were, an idolised replica of himself – one of glittering perfection ... It is the account given by the Deuteronomistic historian which has coloured our picture of the reign of Solomon to date. (Fritz, 1996, p. 188)

Fritz, like Jamieson-Drake, wants to test this picture by archaeological evidence. He picks up the concept of Solomon as a great builder of cities and explores this in relation to archaeological discoveries at the cities of Hazor and Megiddo. There are considerable problems in attributing particular strata to one fixed timespan since all that remains are foundations of buildings, usually without any inscriptional evidence of who built them or why. Fritz, however, unlike Jamieson-Drake, is optimistic about the findings at Hazor and Megiddo:

> Even though only a few cities of the tenth century have been excavated to date, the findings that have been reported do permit some conclusions ... the foundation of new cities in the country was originally connected with the establishment of the kingdom ... (Fritz, 1996, pp. 194–5)

Fritz has accommodated the archaeological discoveries to a biblical account, whereas Jamieson-Drake prefers to critique the biblical story in the light of external evidence. Both scholars agree that the Deuteronomistic version of Solomon's reign deliberately gilds its hero so that glory can shine forth from him and set the kingly ideal. What historical reality lies behind this account? It seems best to assume a gradual development of monarchy towards its climax in the eighth/seventh centuries, since there is more external evidence in terms of written text and artefacts such as seals from this later time to support the view that Israel and Judah had developed by then a form of centralized government.

The kingdoms of Israel and Judah

It does, indeed, seem possible that such a centralised kingship existed in eighth- to seventh-century Israel and Judah. Jamieson-Drake notes the archaeological signs of a rise of a centralized state in the eighth century, its flourishing in the seventh, and its sudden and certain collapse in the sixth century (Jamieson-Drake, 1991, ch. 5). This picture fits with the general Deuteronomistic presentation of kings as continuing after Solomon in two separate kingdoms, Northern and Judahite, until the Assyrian and Babylonian invasions of the seventh and sixth centuries respectively (1 Kings 12 – 2 Kings).

Whereas Judah accepts Rehoboam as king, Jeroboam secedes from that rule and establishes a separate northern kingdom (1 Kgs 12:16–17). Not only did Jeroboam set up a rival kingship, but he also established an independent worship system based on Bethel and Dan, using images of bull calves (1 Kgs 12:25–33). The history of the northen kings now unfolds with a series of uprisings and *coups d'état*. In 1 Kings 16 Omri comes to power, followed by Ahab and later by Jehu. These kings are pictured as struggling to hold on to their land in the face of Syrian threats from rulers such as Ben Hadad, king of Syria (cf. 1 Kgs 20). Finally the exterior forces became strong enough to overcome Israel. 'Then the king of Assyria invaded all the land and came to Samaria . . . in the ninth year of Hoshea the king of Assyria captured Samaria and he carried the Israelites away to Assyria . . .' (2 Kgs 17:6). The history of the northern kingdom ends at this point, but that of Judah continues to the point at which Babylon seizes power over it.

Kings in Israel

The kingdom founded

David and Solomon – Tenth century BCE

The kingdoms divided

North (Israel)	South (Judah)
Jeroboam 1	Rehoboam
Nadab	Abijah
Baasha	Asa
Elah	Jehoshaphat
Zimri	Jehoram
Omri	Amaziah
Ahab	Uzziah (Azariah)
Ahaziah	Jotham
Jehoram	Ahaz
Jehu	*Hezekiah*
Jehoahaz	*Manasseh*
Jehoash	Amon
Jeroboam II	*Josiah*
Zechariah	Jehoahaz II
Shallum	Jehoiakim
Menahem	Jehoiachin
Pekahiah	Zedekiah
Hoshea	

Samaria captured by Assyria	Jerusalem captured by Babylon
Eighth century BCE	Sixth century BCE

These lists mention in order the kings recorded in 1 and 2 Kings. No dates are given since it is extremely difficult to be certain about chronology. This is partly because there are ambiguities in the list such as the fact that some kings appear to have two names, and also because the ancient systems of dating are not expressed in modern terms. Palestinian dating is usually arrived at by comparison with the chronology for Egyptian rulers. See earlier chart on dating in this book. Many of these kings had short reigns and are not of particular significance to the religious message of the books. Those rulers of greater importance for the biblical narratives have been italicized.

The stories of the kings

The same question might be asked about these rulers as was asked about the previous ones. Is there any external evidence of their reigns? Here, at last, there are echoes from outside the biblical text. Although Omri receives only six verses of attention (1 Kgs

16:23–28) in the Deuteronomistic account, he is known as founder of a dynasty from the records of other ancient Near Eastern
states. The Mesha stele, for example, the victory pillar of Mesha,
King of Moab, tells of the oppression of Moab by Israel for forty
years, in the time of Omri and one of his sons. It is clear from this
evidence that Omri was, in historical terms, a king of some
considerable importance locally; in fact the Moab stele confirms,
in general, the story of conflict between Israel and Moab recorded
in 2 Kings 3.

There is also evidence for the last stages of Israel's existence
and its struggles with Assyrian overlords. There exists, for
example, the black basalt tribute pillar of Assyrian source which
shows Jehu, king of Israel, bowing down before his overlord; this
can be set against the stories of Jehu told in 2 Kings. With regard
to the southern kingdom, Judah, there exist stone panels depicting
the capture of Lachish, a Judahite city, by the Assyro-Babylonian
forces, which once adorned the rooms of the victor's palace. (Both
of these items can be viewed at the British Museum, London.)
This evidence supports the biblical story of the fading power of
the divided kingdoms in the face of increased strength in
Mesopotamia.

It appears, then, to be the case that in the eighth to seventh
centuries there were centralized kingdoms in Israel and Judah
which could support a literate elite and a degree of regional power.
It is to this period that the OT attributes the writings of prophets
such as Amos, Hosea and Isaiah, while scholars have generally
regarded the Deuteronomistic Histories themselves as emanating
from this time period, with reshaping at a later date. The opportunity for the development of these Israelite states was the power
vacuum in Syro-Palestine caused by the temporary collapse of
Egypt to the south and Mesopotamia to the north. The rise of first
Assyria and then Babylon returned the area to its normal state of
dependence on its greater neighbours (see Chapter 1 for more
details of the geographical and political features of Palestine).

However, it is not clear, even allowing for these overlaps, that
the biblical account of kings may be regarded as a scientific
investigation of their roles. G. Garbini has pointed out in his work
History and Ideology in Ancient Israel (1986), that there are some
peculiar features of the biblical text. In chapter 3 of his book
Garbini examines 'Stories of the Kings', noting the internal discrepancies of the biblical account. One such discrepancy has
already been mentioned, namely the gap between a victory pillar
showing the Omrides to be a long-term power in the area and a

biblical account which gives only five verses to the founder of the dynasty.

A further issue noted by Garbini is the real identity of the king of Judah called Azariah by the Deuteronomistic writer but Uzziah by the Chronicler, whose reign took place against the backdrop of intense commercial trading in the region, connected with Tyre whose ruler at that time was called Hiram. On the one hand the biblical account of this Judahite king is extremely vague and unfocused, and on the other the account of Hiram of Tyre sounds very like the picture of a Hiram painted as part of Solomon's environment. Garbini argues the case for believing that the writer of Kings has carried out some editing of the reigns of kings in order to show Solomon in a better light as a great king. Having done this, the biblical writer then has little left to say about Azariah/Uzziah.

The Deuteronomistic style

As well as noting factual discrepancies, the reader of 1 and 2 Kings becomes aware of a particular style at work in the text. Rulers are classified as good or bad, not by secular success but by religious significance. The measure is whether kings encouraged a strictly Yahwistic cult or whether they supported worship of a range of deities. This is already at work in the story of Solomon, whose decline is attributed to the leading astray of the king to worship other gods, by his foreign wives (1 Kgs 11). This theme partly accounts for the brusque treatment of Omri by the Deuteronomist in 1 Kings 16:25–26, since he is regarded as a bad king who worshipped the false deity set up by Jeroboam.

Kings such as Hezekiah receive a long treatment because of their goodness, although they are not necessarily strong secular rulers. In Hezekiah's case it is possible to highlight the Deuteronomistic shaping of material, since the account of the siege of Jerusalem by Sennacherib of Assyria is recorded both in 2 Kings and in Assyrian records. In the 2 Kings version the Assyrians claim control of Judah, but Hezekiah gains support from the God of Israel who sends angels to attack the Assyrian army, causing many deaths overnight, leading to the king's retreat from the city. In this version Hezekiah scores a notable victory through a miracle sent by God. In the Assyrian version Sennacherib could easily have taken the city by force, but agreed to take voluntary tribute from Hezekiah who thus acknowledged the Assyrian as his overlord; this is then an Assyrian victory. The reality is probably that it was not a victory as such for either side – some illness affected the army, perhaps, and Hezekiah stopped his rebellion against the Assyrians who were occupied with affairs elsewhere in their empire anyway. The focus in 2 Kings, though, is on the manner in which God intervenes in history to support those who pledge themselves and their peoples to worship only the God of Israel. Hezekiah is really a vassal of a great empire but features in the Deuteronomistic History as a great king of Judah.

The Deuteronomistic writers were ambivalent about Israel's response from the start, as can be seen in Judges where the people constantly fall away from God and are defeated by their enemies until a new inspired leader emerges.There are clearly variants on this theme since, in Judges, it is the people who sin while leaders bring them back and, in Kings, it is leaders who are the cause of sin, but there is continuity of thought across these texts, nonetheless. It is this stylistic control of individual scenes as they are made into a collective whole which has led scholars such as Noth to assert the existence of a Deuteronomistic school of editing which viewed all of Israel's past as centred on religious values.

This approach to the texts from Joshua to 2 Kings moves the search for understanding of the texts from a historical to a theological plane, a move which will be addressed in the third section of this book. It also highlights the nature of the text as artistic communication between writer and reader, a theme to be explored in the second section. At this point, however, some summary remarks need to be made concerning the historical aspect of these Deuteronomistic texts.

Biblical archaeology

The first subject needing to be summarized is that of the function of modern archaeology in relation to the OT. The previous chapters have consistently turned to archaeological evidence as a check on the biblical account. Biblical archaeology is a subject which has emerged in the last two hundred years, among Europeans. H. O. Thompson has outlined the development of archaeological technique (Thompson, 1987) from the first attempts to trace ancient sites which were fed by a desire for treasure from the past, to a gradual refinement of processes through the work of archaeologists such as Flinders Petrie (nineteenth century), Mortimer Wheeler and Kathleen Kenyon (twentieth century). The remains of large settlements contain layer upon layer of debris from the past; the task is to separate off each layer at a time, so digging often takes place in small squares and involves careful sifting of soil and dust by hand, using a sieve to track down the smallest fragments of pot or bone. In the twentieth century scientific methods of investigation have broadened to take in aerial photography and carbon dating, for instance (see Thompson, 1987, section 3). As a result of this type of investigation in Syro-Palestine, a great amount of material has been produced. A good deal of it is in the Israel Museum in Jerusalem as well as in museums in countries of archaelogists' origin such as the British Museum, London.

There is, of course, a basic problem with all this material. It is largely non-written, non-textual and so cannot be compared directly with the picture of affairs presented in the OT, which is written and textual. As has been shown, this reality has led to a variety of approaches among scholars. There is the line of argument which says that silence in the material remains about a key biblical figure must be allowed to put the biblical story in doubt as 'accurate history'. On the other hand, there are scholars who argue that what remains, materially, is only a small part of what originally existed and as there is no logic attached to what has survived other than the nature of the materials themselves (papyrus does not last well in the cool, damp climate of Palestine, for instance), silence does not mean the non-existence of a particular figure from the past.

One example will illustrate the issue here. A number of seals have been found which are dated to the eighth to sixth centuries BCE. These seals often have an inscription on them showing to whom they belonged. Three of the seals bear names which are similar to names of characters in biblical stories concerned with the 'Gedaliah incident'. This story is to be found in 2 Kings 25:22–26 and at greater length in Jeremiah 40:7–41:15. It is set in the time when the Babylonians have become the rulers of Judah and have appointed a governor to carry out their rule, a man called Gedaliah. Judah was not yet completely tied down by Babylon, and a conspiracy arose to assassinate Gedaliah and rebel against foreign control. The leader of this group, the one appointed to kill the governor, was Ishmael and the Jeremiah passage states that he had the backing of Baalis, king of the Ammonites. The three seals bear names which appear to link with these three characters, Gedaliah, Ishmael and Baalis. It might, then, be possible to argue that this is material evidence in support of the biblical story as 'real history'. But Becking (in Grabbe (ed.), 1997, pp. 65–83), for instance, thinks not. For a start, there are five different Gedaliahs mentioned in the OT itself and the name may well have been generally popular and given to many men who are not recorded there. Therefore, this Gedalyahu could be someone unconnected with the story in 2 Kings 25. As to the other two seals, one of which refers to Yishma'el and the other to Baalys, the same may well be true of them, although Baalis is not a common biblical name. And even if the seals did belong to the figures behind the 2 Kings story, a further problem occurs:

> Even if it could be proved that Gdlyhw, Yshm"l and B'lysh' are indeed identical with Gedaliah, Ismael and Baalis, this does not prove the historicity of the Gedaliah incident. The inscriptions can make clear that persons by that name actually lived in the period under consideration . . . That . . . does not imply that acts pursued by those individuals as reported . . . in later narratives are thus historical. (Becking, 1997, p. 83)

What, then, can be said of biblical archaeology? It does not solve all historical problems for the biblicist and it does not fill in all the gaps in historical knowledge connected with the biblical account. On the other hand, it is the true companion of biblical study. The ancient texts surfaced within cultures whose material remains are now partially available to the biblical student. Despite methodological tensions, the two lines of study and research belong with each other.

The history of Israel

The second topic to be summarized is that of history itself. To modern readers the books from Joshua to 2 Kings appear to be history books. That is, they appear to record the events of the past. It has become clear already that this is an imprecise understanding of the purpose of the books. They relate to events in the past and they construct narratives about those events. They tell the tale of the past and should, therefore, be labelled historiography. Historiography is writing about the past in the light of a modern writer's understanding of what the significance of the past events was. Individual scenes are brought together in a manner which gives purpose to the past.

Since the Deuteronomistic books are works of historiography can they validly be used by modern historians as primary resource material for modern accounts of biblical Israel? This question is reflected in the title of a recent book edited by L. Grabbe, *Can a 'History of Israel' Be Written?* (1997). In this volume a number of historians of the ancient world express their views on this subject. These opinions range from cautious optimism that writing something accurate about ancient Israel is a valid enterprise to controlled scepticism about any such endeavour. One of the major issues is the tension between the two main sources of information for a modern historian, archaeology and biblical text – a subject which has been addressed above.

The second issue relates to the definition of the biblical histories as historiography rather than raw data. Thus they are not the 'stuff of history' from which writings about the past can be constructed; they are themselves literary constructions of stories about the past. What actually happened within the developing society of ancient Israel is no longer straightforwardly accessible to the modern reader of the Deuteronomistic texts. If modern scholars are to use these texts as a resource for their own accounts of early Israel, care has to be taken not only to identify the bias brought to such a work by a twentieth-century writer, but also the bias brought to the task by the ancient historiographer. The meaning of any written text from the past will have been shaped by the perspective of its original writer (cf. Barstad, in Grabbe (ed.), 1997, pp. 37–64).

K. Whitelam's book *The Invention of Ancient Israel* (1996) has highlighted the way in which ancient meanings may not be sufficiently identified in their own right and so may be, uncritically, absorbed into the creation of a modern understanding of the events described by the ancient text, and may be used as part of modern meanings given to the text. But what is actually produced is a theoretical evaluation of the past in two stages – what one set of ancient writers made of ancient Israel combined with what one set of modern writers made of the ancient writers' picture of the past.

So can anyone validly write biblical history? On this matter L. Grabbe offers a buoyant approach. Biblical text can and must be used. There is not enough archaeological data as such, so biblical material is vital, though the difficulties of using biblical text should not be under-estimated. The various types of sources need to be evaluated on their own before any synthesis is attempted and the lines of approach taken by a modern historian, using these sources, should be made absolutely clear. The historian's own cultural position must be stated and should be taken into account wherever that person's work is evaluated (Grabbe, 1997, p. 36).

History as Story

6

Narrative art and the Deuteronomistic Histories

In the first section of this book attention was focused on the historical issues relating to the texts from Joshua to 2 Kings. Since the Deuteronomistic texts appear to be a history of Israel, questions can reasonably be asked about what kind of history this is and how its contents fit in with historical information about Syro-Palestine drawn from archaeological sources. In the course of asking such questions it became clear that the status of the books from Joshua to 2 Kings as historical resources for research into ancient Israel is not firmly established. They cannot be read as 'history' as such but have to be treated as ancient historiographical accounts of an even more ancient past.

Since there is no consensus as to the weight to be placed on the Deuteronomistic Histories, different scholars produce different messages about their meaning. Yet the goal of an historical-critical approach to the Deuteronomistic texts is to arrive at 'the truth' about ancient Israel. It should be possible to produce a single interpretation of the text which compels acceptance among all readers of the relevant material. The failure, in practice, to find such a compelling account of ancient Israel has led to disenchantment and frustration among scholars concerning the use of historical methods of investigation to interpret Joshua to 2 Kings. This has led, in turn, to the search for alternative methods of reading and researching the Deuteronomistic Histories.

The movement away from historical-critical interpretation of the Bible has produced a variety of alternative methodologies, each of which has its own structure and its own practitioners; all of these methodologies have equal value since each produces its own type of truth. No longer is there a focus on one, single, absolute truth, rather a variety of parallel, independent truths are brought to the reader's attention.

Alternative ideologies

The historical-critical method focused on the search for the original value of biblical texts in their ancient setting. This has given way to a postmodern exploration of the diversity and variety of possible meanings for OT books. These styles have been investigated in, for instance, *The Post Modern Bible* (1995), in which each chapter has been written collectively by a group of scholars interested in that particular methodology. There are chapters on:

- reader response criticism
- structural and narratological criticism
- post-structuralist criticism
- psychoanalytical criticism
- feminist and womanist criticism
- ideological criticism

Each of these topics produces a separate research method. Reader response looks at the manner in which readers respond to text, how a text engages its readers. Structuralist, post-structuralist and rhetorical criticism all relate to the literary format of a text. Is it in the style of a folktale, for instance, or a fable? What literary techniques are employed in a text to persuade readers of the value of the text's message? Psychoanalytical criticism applies the theories of psychology, such as those of Freud, to literature, which is thus viewed as the reflection of the human psyche. Feminist criticism has become such a major method of biblical research that a whole chapter of this present book will deal with feminist investigation of the Deuteronomistic texts. Ideological criticism deals with the overall attitudes or principles to which a text relates and by which it is shaped.

In producing this collective volume the authors of *The Post Modern Bible* intend to show modern readers how the Bible, a book of considerable formative influence on European culture, is relevant not only for its witness to the ancient past, but for its ongoing potential influence on society:

> We are . . . arguing for a *transforming* biblical criticism, one that undertakes to understand the ongoing impact of the Bible in culture and one that . . . benefits from the rich resources of contemporary thought in language, epistemology, method, rhetorical power, . . . gender, race, class, sexuality and, indeed, religion – which have come to occupy centre stage in discourses both public and academic.
> (Bible Collective, 1995, p. 2)

Postmodernity and Judges

Judges and Method (1995), edited by G. Yee, adopts a number of the approaches discussed in *The Post Modern Bible* and applies them to the book of Judges. The purpose here is twofold, to illustrate how modern biblical research methods operate in practice and to produce fresh insights into the meaning of Judges itself. Scholars with an expertise in a particular methodology contribute to the chapters of this volume which moves through narrative criticism of Judges, to social-scientific criticism, to feminist criticism, to structuralist and deconstructive methods, to ideological criticism.

Each contributor introduces

> the approach by examining the presuppositions of the method: the particular questions it asks of the text and its central characteristics . . . The contributor then . . . [applies] the method to the book of Judges, either to the text as a whole or certain selections. (in Yee (ed.), 1995, p. 12)

R. Bowman's chapter focuses on narrative criticism. According to Bowman 'Narrative criticism seeks to discover and disclose the narrative's own intrinsic points of emphasis (Bowman, 1995, p. 17). This approach assumes that the final form of the text operates as a coherent story which exists in its own right as a literary piece and which, when analysed by literary tools, will reveal the particular perspective of its author.

The literary tools to be used include an assessment of the role of the narrator who tells the story, of the links between the structure of narrated story and scenes of dialogue which are inserted into that framework, of narrative structure and plot, and of characterization. Bowman discusses each of these literary devices as they may be found in Judges before turning to an overall investigation of the book through the eyes of a narrative critic.

Bowman argues that the fundamental subject of Judges is the relationship between God and the Hebrew people, taking God and people here to be the equivalent of two characters in a story. 'God and the Hebrew people are directly conveyed through the narrator's comments and evaluations' (Bowman, 1995, p. 21). The structuring of the narrative provides an interpretation of the God–people relationship in which God is viewed as one who intervenes to punish transgressions. The phrase the people 'did what was evil in the sight of the Lord' is repeated at critical points in the story, where the fortunes of the people are at a low ebb. On each occasion the phrase introduces the intervention of God in the story, to enact punishment on Israel through her enemies (Bowman, 1995, p. 32). This narrative pattern is balanced by the picture of God as one who delivers from oppression. Each time the people are threatened by enemies, God raises up a saviour; so the individual story of each judge is inserted into a broader narrative framework which gives added meaning to the accounts of the judge's heroic acts.

The broad framework in turn involves a combination of divine action and human response. The text speaks of God as 'with his people', or 'with X' (as in Judg 6:12, 16). A parallel theme is that of the conferral of God's spirit on a chosen person. Both Gideon and Jephthah, for instance, have aid from the divine spirit. But in each case human response also has a part in the story. Gideon demands extra assurances of divine assistance and Jephthah makes a vow of sacrifice in return for divine aid (Bowman, 1995, p. 37). In Jephthah's case, especially, human response is treated ambiguously in the narrative, since his need to persuade God to be with him leads to his daughter's death. God, however, does not intervene to change or limit human response; the vow once made has to be paid.

The narrative tension between divine and human activity in Judges is emphasized in the story of Samson. God is the cause of Samson's birth and God's spirit is with the child (Judg 13:24–25). Samson is able to perform prodigious acts of strength and so to be a threat to the Philistines. But he limits his own power through intimacy with foreign women, one of whom, Delilah, worms out of him the secret of his power i.e. his uncut hair. Samson thus jeopardizes his own power, loses God's spirit and becomes weak. Yet as his hair grows divine power returns to him and his final human choice of destruction brings down his people's enemies as well. This narrative structure suggests a direct linking of God's role and human action:

> Divine success appears contingent upon an appropriate human response. Hence, the exercise of divine power is limited by the exercise of human freedom, the exercise of which frequently misuses and abuses human potential . . . God will act to punish transgressions, but not to prevent them. (Bowman, 1995, p. 39)

Bowman's examination of narrative structures in the book of Judges as a whole, with regard to God and the people as two major 'characters' of the text, highlights the interplay between literary style and meaning or message. In this view the structuring of the text serves to convey meaning; analysing the structure enables the reader to see that meaning more clearly. But, conversely, it is the need to convey this particular meaning which has led the writer to employ the particular literary devices found in this text. Structure promotes meaning and meaning shapes structure. Arriving at this conclusion involves the reader of Judges in an acceptance that the book forms a single coherent narrative, on the one hand, and, on the other, in an awareness of how individual short stories are incorporated into the overarching narrative structure.

The methodology of narrative criticism

Bowman's article on narrative criticism in Judges illustrates the way in which, in postmodernity, literary methodologies have emerged as major scholarly methods of researching texts. This method of investigation is defined as synchronic (at the same time) reading. The book to be read is considered to be essentially one single work, although it may be made up of a number of individual chapters or sections. A more historical reading of biblical texts assumes that the final form of the book is the work of a series of ancient editors who reshaped existing material, either written or oral; books should, then, be taken apart into their component elements.

By contrast, narrative criticism looks to the way in which the many subordinate parts of a book impinge on one another, so building up the final message which a reader takes away. It is possible to examine the technique of the writer and evaluate how skilfully linguistic devices are used. The main aspects of this style of literary criticism concern the roles of narrator, plot, characters and language skills such as wordplay and metaphor. The purpose of these three chapters is to explore aspects of narrative criticism as these have been applied to the Deuteronomistic Histories. In this chapter the intention is to give some basic information about the narrative-critical style and then to examine narrative criticism of 1 Kings as an example of this method at work on the Deuteronomistic texts.

What is narrative art?

Narrative criticism is a method of exploring the manner in which narratives (stories) are written. A narrative presupposes the role of narrator, often an anonymous figure in biblical books, who tells the story. Insofar as the narrator shapes the story, by telling it, the narrator represents the author of the story. However, the author is separate from the narrator since the author chooses how the narrator is to operate within a given story. The story has a plot, a story line, with a beginning which introduces the persons and issues to be dealt with, a middle in which people interact in a series of situations, and an end where tensions created in the story are resolved. The simplest narrative structure is the form

> Once upon a time there were . . . and . . .
> but . . . so they all lived happily ever after.

Given this narrative framework, a reader can study both the plot and the characters engaged in the action of the plot, with regard to the skilfulness with which the author presents and interweaves these elements of the story. Finally the linguistic structures of the text can be investigated. In the case of the Hebrew Bible this entails examination of the structures of Hebrew narrative style and the devices of the Hebrew language.

Narrative art and the Hebrew Bible

The Literary Guide to the Bible (1987), edited by R. Alter and F. Kermode is a foundation text in the area of narrative criticism. Chapter by chapter it provides a literary commentary on separate books of the Christian Bible and so gives literary commentary a standing equal to that of historical commentaries:

> The coming together of religious and secular criticisms has taught practitioners of the former that their studies may be greatly enhanced by attention to secular methods; the latter have benefitted by discovering that the Bible, to which few of the most influential critics had of late paid much attention, is simply of such quality that they have neglected it to their immense cost. (Alter and Kermode, p. 3)

More recently D. M. Gunn and D. N. Fewell have produced *Narrative Art in the Hebrew Bible* (1993). This work addresses the issues of character, plot and language as they relate to the Hebrew Bible. In each instance a broad introduction to the feature concerned is linked with an interpretation of a specific biblical text employing that feature. Thus consideration of characters and narrators is allied to a study of Tamar and Judah in Genesis 38 and that of plot to Judges 10–12. In this latter treatment the authors point out that 'because most stories involve more than one character it is not uncommon to see several desires, often in conflict, working themselves out' (Gunn and Fewell, 1993, p. 112).

This comment can be related to plot in the story of Jephthah's daughter in Judges 10–12. Jephthah operates on the public stage of national affairs. He wants victory in war and vows to God a sacrifice of the first person he meets on returning from battle, if he wins. But the first person he meets is someone from the private sphere of home life, his own daughter. The conflicting fields of public and private events are interwoven; the hero of national victory must grieve as parent for the loss of his own child. Jephthah's daughter has her own agenda too, and takes the lead role from her father, taking charge of her own affairs in the face of death.

Another significant study of *Narrative Art in the Hebrew Bible* is that of Shimon Bar-Efrat (2nd edn 1989) who deals with narrator, characters, plot, time and space and style. General discussion of these subjects is illustrated by examples from biblical narrative. In relation to time Bar-Efrat notes:

> Because of the consecutive nature of language, which is the means by which works of literature are conveyed, the narrative cannot be absorbed all at once and is communicated through a process which continues in time . . . (Bar-Efrat, 1989, p. 141)

The writer can speed up this time process or slow it down, in order to produce meaning. In the story of the rape of Tamar, David's daughter (2 Sam 13:1–22), by her half-brother Amnon, time is distributed fairly evenly over all the events narrated (Bar-Efrat, 1989, p. 280). This allows the author to make it clear to the reader that what happens before and after the rape are more important than the rape itself. The author dwells on all the preparations for the rape and the reactions to it, while reporting the actual deed in telegraphic terms; this leads us to infer that the emphasis in this narrative is on the human and psychological aspects of events rather than on factual facets (Bar-Efrat, 1989, p. 280).

1 Kings and narrative commentary

Building on the continuing interest in narrative criticism a new series of biblical commentaries is being published to focus on literary rather than on historical comments, while still using the typical commentary format – an indepth study of a particular biblical text as a whole and in its component parts, including linguistic skills.

J. T. Walsh has contributed the volume on 1 Kings (1996). This study commences with an introduction which lays down the critical methods the author will apply in the commentary proper. These include the common elements of narrator, plot and characterization; the commentator also draws attention to the role of linguistic features in creation of meaning. Hebrew narratives are marked by a particular tense of the verb, called by scholars the story-telling tense, which begins each new story 'And it was that . . .' (Hebrew: *wayyictol*). The Hebrew language does not subordinate clauses on the whole, so events are usually linked by a simple conjunction 'and . . . and . . .' which may sometimes be translated as 'but' in English. It is left to the reader to subordinate one idea to the next, one narrated event to the next, and so reach meaning. Hebrew prose is, to that extent, open ended and capable of several interpretations. Further meaning is arrived at by word-play – the repetition of words or sounds with similar shape or sounding. Solomon's name (Hebrew: *Sh-l-m-h*) is played upon in the scene where Ahijah tears his garment (Hebrew: *S-l-m-h*) into twelve pieces to demonstrate the tearing apart of Solomon's kingdom in the future (1 Kgs 11:29–32) (Walsh, 1996, p. xvi). Repetition of phrases also marks beginnings and endings of sub-sections of text and allows key features of the structure to emerge.

Thus, as Walsh points out, 1 Kings 2:31–33 communicates its meaning by the use of a repeated theme, a parallelism in the text technically called chiasm, in which the fate of David's house begins and ends the subsection. The reader can analyse how phrases bounded by this repetition balance one another, leaving the ignorance of David concerning Joab's murders as the focal point. This highlights Joab's guilt and David's innocence.

> A David's house will be freed of bloodguilt (2:31b)
>   B punishment will fall on Joab's head (2:32a)
>   C he killed two men better than himself (2:32b)
>   D my father David did not know it (2:32c)
>   C* Abner and Amasa (2:32d)
>   B* their blood will be on Joab's head (2:33a)
> A* David's house will have peace (2:33b) (Walsh, 1996, p. 58)

1 Kings 2:28–35 is the wider context in which the above passage can be found. It is concerned with the story of Solomon's relationship with Joab and how Solomon achieves the death of Joab. The scene opens with Joab's flight to sanctuary when he hears how

Solomon is moving against his potential enemies. Since he clings to the altar Solomon's servant is reluctant to kill him as his master has ordered, lest he commit sacrilege. But Solomon points out that Joab is himself a murderer who has brought bloodguilt on David's house since he committed murder as David's servant, and so justifies the killing of one who is unworthy of sanctuary since he is not an innocent man. Walsh's analysis of the short passage from the middle of this text shows how the literary structures of the text work, in detail, to move a narrative towards its conclusion.

Walsh's commentary frequently addresses the use of parallelisms in the text of 1 Kings, both in short passages and in larger sections such as the first eleven chapters of the book. 1 Kings 1–11 contains the story of Solomon, told from his rise to power as an adult, one of David's sons, to his gradual decline in power and death. Walsh suggests (1996, p. 151) that the entire eleven chapters of the Solomon story are shaped by a balancing structure which leaves the building and consecration of the Temple as the hinge of the narrative, constituting the climax of the story and the high point of royal power. In the first part of the narrative Solomon is shown as a man inheriting a kingdom, pacifying it, ruling it well and honouring the national god. In the parallel second half the same themes occur but with a different slant. Solomon now uses his gifts for his own enhancement, burdening the northern tribes with heavy taxes, while his marriages to foreign wives cause him to worship other gods. The glory of his reign fades in the face of threats to his rule from human beings and divine rejection of him as king.

The message conveyed through this literary structure is further enhanced by the use of characterization. In the first chapters Solomon is, on the surface, applauded as a character. But closer reading of the text reveals hints of doubt concerning his heroic stature, deconstructing the main message and foreshadowing the ultimate failure of the reign. This characterization draws in the role of the narrrator who tells the story:

> On the surface he depicts Solomon positively: his decisions are always justified, and sometimes they are even merciful. But beneath the surface the narrator uses a variety of subtle narrative devices to suggest a different, much more negative picture. (Walsh, 1996, p. 65)

Solomon, for instance, acts swiftly and sensibly to secure his own position versus Adonijah who has claimed David's throne. But the reader is left to consider the ruthless manner in which Solomon disposes of his political enemies, by manipulating situations such as Joab's guilt to bring about the extermination of hostile rivals for power in the kingdom.

Walsh's commentary explores the intricacies of narrative style which interweave to produce a range of meanings hidden in the text of 1 Kings, and which are made accessible for the reader through a research method based on literary format and linguistic structure. The bottom line for this research is the Hebrew language itself: a fact which reminds the reader that the ultimate foundation of communication is the use of words and their meanings. Since a word stands in for some other reality – 'table', for instance, for a particular physical object, or 'cat' for a specific and recognizable animal – it is to be treated as a symbol or signpost for that other reality. But different experiences of reality may lead to different undertsandings about the meaning which a particular word conveys. When I hear the word 'table' what do I envisage? A solid wooden rectangle on four legs? A transparent glass circle resting on a metal support? Or . . .? It may be that I recognize a range of different objects as all symbolized by the word 'table', but it may also be that the term conjures up for me only one particular object while it leads another person to envisage a second individual item. The question then arises as to whether effective communication can take place between myself and that other person even if we use the same words since those words carry different meanings for each of us.

These problems of human communication are linked to the origins of language. Each language system has its own vocabulary built up from the cultural, everyday experiences of the group whose communication system it is. Translation of words from language to language is already interpretation, since the new word may not carry exactly the same value in its linguistic setting as the original word did in its own language context. Some words have no exact equivalent in another language and may be imported as a loan-word – as in the French borrowing of 'Le Weekend' from English culture, for instance. Or some existing word may be pressed into a new function, given new meanings as the translation of a foreign word.

The use of language

Studies of biblical literature involve, then, the consideration of how language works as a communication tool. How language works is the subject of the discipline of semiotics, the study of language as symbolic of other realities (Greek: *sémeion*). G. Aichele has published an introduction to the relevance of semiotics for biblical study, called *Text, Sign and Scripture* (1997). The fundamental layer of scriptural text and interpretation is the interaction between reader and text. This is not an easy relationship since it involves indirect communication. If two people are engaged in conversation they can check out their understanding of the words used in their dialogue by asking questions of each other. But the authors of biblical texts are not available for a reader who wishes to check out the meaning of words in biblical passages and why these particular words are used:

> Scholarly research may identify historical or cultural features of people who produced the various biblical texts . . . However, in the last analysis, the senders of these texts are no better known to us than the mysterious voice on the other end of the phoneline . . . (Aichele, 1997, p. 27)

On top of this obstacle to understanding words in a text there is the further problem caused by translation. 'Given the difficulties, risks and uncertainties that attend every translation, no translation can be free from the translator's theological or ideological bias . . .' (Aichele, 1997, p. 55).

The focus in interpretation of language in a text moves, because of these issues, from the message signified by words to the words, the signifiers, themselves. Language is produced by particular people in a given society and is shaped by the lifestyle and historical experiences of that society. Take, for example, the frequent use of the term 'Israel' in the Deuteronomistic Histories, particularly in phrases such as 'The people of Israel did what was evil in the sight of the Lord' (Judg 6:1). A modern reader encountering that term in a text may well bring a range of meanings to bear in order to arrive at its significance. On the one hand it may link with a current world religion and in particular a country connected with that religion. But this is not the same social and political reality as that conveyed by the use of the term on the Merneptah stele of the thirteenth-century BCE, even though that reference also appears to have been to a particular place or people. A Christian modern reader may be aware that Israel was used in the Pauline Letters of the New Testament to refer to God's kingdom, the cultural home of Christians and so this reader will interpret the broader meaning of the Deuteronomistic text as having something to say to a Christian sense of identity. These few examples do not, of course, exhaust the range of meaning which attaches to the word 'Israel', but they serve to illustrate the complex system of values conveyed by the term. But how is the word to be read when it occurs in Judges? It must, ultimately, take its meaning from the world, the universe, of that text itself.

'Israel' may mean many things, but in the Deuteronomistic works it implies the existence of All-Israel. Although there are geographical and political overtones here, the main meaning is religious. Israel is primarily a congregation of people for divine worship and even their daily life is meant to reflect that basic truth. Israel as a term has two faces here. On the one hand it is the sign of divine power and authority, the All-Israel intended to be God's people; on the other hand it is the kingdom which human beings have made for themselves and which sometimes is at odds with the God of Israel, when its leaders worship other deities and neglect YHWH.

Summary

This chapter has explored the broad area of narrative criticism within the variety of modern biblical exegetical methods. It is clearly a major method of interpreting biblical text and can itself be subdivided into individual tools for constructing effective stories. So far the broad outline of the methodology has been established; in the other two chapters in this section some particular features of narrative investigation of the Deuteronomistic works will be undertaken.

7

Tragedy and history

The previous chapter introduced the reader to the concept of narrative criticism in relation to the OT. In the course of that chapter it was pointed out that the application of narrative criticism to texts requires the use of literary tools derived from the nature of story – hence plot, characterization, the role of the narrator. A further dimension of narrative critique concerns the mood of the story – specifically whether this is comic or tragic. In tragic mood there is no happy resolution of tensions and the emphasis is on fragmentation and the frustration of human purposes for good. The narrative leaves the reader face to face with the unanswerable problems of human anguish and suffering.

The nature of tragedy

In the literary context 'tragedy' is a technical name for one particular style. The term derives from theatre in ancient Greece, where the plays of Aeschylus, Sophocles and Euripides provide the basic patterns for tragic drama. In addition, Aristotle, in his *Poetics*, attempted to define the nature of tragedy by philosophical argument. These ancient literary forms have been used by modern literary critics as a means of evaluating Western literature, Shakespeare's plays for instance.

> There is in the final moments of great tragedy . . . a fusion of grief and joy, of lament over the fall of man and of rejoicing in the resurrection of his spirit. (Steiner, 1961, p. 10)

The model has at its core the fact of catastrophe: 'any realistic notion of tragic drama must start from the fact of catastrophe. Tragedies end badly' (Steiner, 1961, p. 8). The disaster is not predictable in ordinary terms, rather it comes upon the scene of human affairs apparently in a wholly random manner. It dominates the events of the drama, however, forcing the human characters to engage with total darkness and distress. It would be possible to situate Job 3 in this context since, at this point, Job has no hope left and curses his own day of birth, wishing to release upon it the powers of chaos.

Steiner, however, would disagree since Job is a biblical book and as such is part of a collection wherein God is ultimately in charge of affairs. This deity is presented as authoritative and capable of rational control of world affairs. For Steiner this rules out tragedy in the true sense. 'Jehovah is just, even in his fury . . . over the sum of time, there can be no doubt that the ways of God to man are just' (Steiner, 1961, p. 4). C. Exum, however, disagrees with Steiner at this point, arguing that biblical material is truly tragic at times:

> In the Bible, the association of good and evil within the divine provides fertile ground for tragic awareness to grow . . . If Saul's deterioration were entirely his own doing or if Jephthah's vow were a premeditated decision, the tragic power of these stories would be greatly diminished. (Exum, 1992, p. 9)

It is Exum's viewpoint, rather than Steiner's, which is the basis for this present chapter.

The tragic hero

A focus for tragic events is the life of one human being, a great hero whose rise and fall are conveyed in the plot of the tragedy. This emphasis on the achievements and losses of a single character is the meaning given to tragedy in Chaucer's *Canterbury Tales*, a definition which is to be found in the prologue to the Monk's tale. Shakespeare's plays contain a number of such figures, especially that of King Lear. Originally a man of great authority, priding himself on wise judgement and honesty, Lear is deceived by his trust in his daughters and finds himself powerless at their hands. Maddened by his suffering, Lear wanders the countryside accompanied by his court fool, finding peace with his youngest daughter before his career ends in death. Here is an archetype of a great man whose fatal flaws bring him down to sickness and death.

It is possible to compare biblical characters with this model of the tragic hero. Job, in chapters 3–41 of the book, acts as such a figure though he does not directly create his own suffering. It could be argued, nonetheless, that Job's careful piety is rather complacent, allowing him to believe in future prosperity on the strength of his religious practices (Job 1). In the Deuteronomistic texts Saul and David are both candidates for the role of tragic hero.

The stories of Saul and David as tragic narrative

Saul's story is to be found in 1 Samuel 9–31, chapters which tell of the rise of the institution of kingship in Israel. Saul's reign seems hopeful; he is young, strong and handsome, also full of YHWH's spirit. But not for long; the first promise fades as Saul lives out his role as leader. He allows himself to be sidetracked from his pursuit of the enemy into a diplomatic battle with David. From chapter 16 God rejects Saul, whose mind is increasingly distorted by an evil spirit. This rejection eventually leads to Saul's death in battle. In this story the contrasting of Saul's strengths and his weaknesses allows the reader to view the tale as tragic in tone.

David's story occupies more space in 1 and 2 Samuel than does Saul's. David also begins as a young handsome figure full of promise as a leader. He manages to survive both a personal contest with the Philistine champion (1 Sam 17) and Saul's hatred (1 Sam 18 onwards). He succeeds Saul as king and unites all the tribes of Israel under his authority, finally bringing the Ark of the Lord to rest in his new capital city of Jerusalem (2 Sam 6). But David's adultery with Bathsheba and subsequent murder of her husband mark the turn of fortune's wheel. David now begins a slow decline marked especially by the revolt of his son Absalom, leading to civil war and the death of Absalom. Once again the contrasting of strength and weakness in the character of the king allows the reader to view this narrative as a tragic piece of literature.

It is these elements of the Saul and David narratives which have been picked up by C. Exum in her book *Tragedy and Biblical Narrative* (1992). Exum regards the stories of Saul and David as examples of tragedy in the OT. Saul, risen to greatness, refuses to abandon his kingship:

> Caught between his own turbulent personality and the antagonism of God toward human kingship . . . [he] displays heroic greatness in his refusal to acquiesce in the fate prophesied by Samuel . . . A lesser man . . . might merely accept his destiny. Saul, however, wrestles against it.' (Exum, 1992, p. 41)

David's story also contains a tragic dimension:

We find it in the reversal of the hero's fortunes that takes place as a
result of his sins, in the suggestions of hostile transcendence that
accompany David's guilt, and in the series of unmitigated disasters
that beset the Davidic house. (Exum, 1992, p. 142)

In order to investigate how the theme of tragedy is played out in
the narratives of these two men, attention will now be given to two
incidents each of which highlights the tragic circumstances of the
central character in the story.

1 Samuel 28

In this chapter the story is told of Saul's preparations for his final
campaign. Saul is still officially king over Israel and its military
chief. But the reader knows that God has long since abandoned
Saul and given his own spirit to David instead. An evil spirit
troubles Saul making him depressed and suspicious. Faced with
Philistine preparations for war he is nervous and unsure. This
characterization of the hero reflects the stage of the hero's decline.
At the start of his career Saul fearlessly gathered the Israelites for
battle against their enemies (1 Sam 11), but now he trembles and
is afraid. The death of Samuel has deprived him of a prophetic
word from God and other methods of obtaining divine guidance
have failed, as indicated in verse 6. All the signs are that Saul's
entry into battle will be disastrous.

Abandoned by God, Saul clings to his old power and makes a
final attempt to seek supernatural aid. In the crisis he turns to
religious practitioners whose work he had himself outlawed. In
this way he abandons his own identity, just as he also disguises
himself and goes in darkness and in secret to consult the medium.
This tragic Saul moves away from his familiar course and stands
outside his previous social role. The scene plays on Saul's lack of
identity. The woman is afraid to bring up a spirit for him because
the king (i.e. Saul) has forbidden such an act. Only when Saul
swears an oath by the very God whom he is abandoning in this
attempt to seek help, is the woman reassured. Here dramatic irony
serves to emphasize the tragic overtones of the scene.

But Saul's anonymity vanishes as Samuel is raised. When the
woman recognizes that it is Samuel who comes she also recognizes
the king. Saul's evil destiny now comes towards its climax. Samuel
comes from the earth to proclaim a final prophecy of doom against
him from the Lord of Israel (verse 17). Israel also will suffer with
its king as, on the morrow, all will be given up by God into the

hands of the Philistines. The atmosphere of this scene is one of fear and awe. Saul is desperate, the woman terribly afraid of punishment, Samuel's appearance from the ground is godlike as he thunders a doom on the now terrified king. Saul has been pushed to the extremities of feeling and left with no hope. Thus a totally tragic mood is created within the narrative. In the rest of the scene the tragic tension is eased as the woman performs an act of kindness from one human being to a suffering neighbour, persuading the king to eat. But this lessening of tension also confirms the inevitable tragedy which will be fulfilled in the last scene of Saul's story where Saul dies on the field of battle, resisting the Philistines to the last.

2 Samuel 15

In this chapter David's son Absalom secretly gathers an army for himself, in a great conspiracy to seize the throne from his father, David. In verse 13 news is brought to David of Absalom's activity. David calls on his household to flee in order to escape capture by Absalom. Thus a great king whose word has gone out from his capital Jerusalem to command the tribes of Israel is now forced by fate to flee his own centre of power, with only his household, in a haste that prevents the gathering of possessions. Ironically, in verse 16, the mighty man of past battles leaves ten concubines to keep his house; ten women, second-class citizens in the OT, take the place of a great king. Thus the tragic theme, how the mighty are fallen, is fleshed out in the narrative.

Pathos is introduced to the story as David leaves his city. Ittai, a foreigner, refuses to abandon the king – an implicit contrast with David's own son who has rejected him. David had shown great commitment in the past to the God of Israel, bringing the Ark to rest in Jerusalem. Now priests bring the Ark to preside over David's departure from the city. But the Ark, too, must be left behind. David knows he may never see it again (verse 26). References to people weeping as they watch the king depart are picked up in verse 30, but now it is the king who weeps.

The narrator of the scene thus emphasizes the total weakness and dependence of a man who had previously been in total command of other people's lives. Separated from all but his household, David is met on the one hand by Mephibosheth's kindness and on the other by Shimei's curses. Tragic events have made him a passive figure. He accepts food from one and cursing from the other, for both of these represent the fate that God has appointed for him: 'Behold, my own son seeks my life; how much more now may this Benjamite! Let him alone, and let him curse; for the Lord has bidden him' (2 Sam 16:11). In this moment of total loss and pain, David bows his head before destiny and learns the tragic lesson of the illusory nature of human strength and pride.

Saul and David: tragic heroes?

These scenes offer the reader evidence for viewing Saul and David as tragic heroes. Each man is assailed by evil yet takes steps to cope with the disaster, while at the same time knowing that the God who has turned events against them cannot be overcome by merely human efforts. But are Saul and David tragic heroes in the fullest sense? T. R. Preston in 'The heroism of Saul . . .' (in Exum (ed.), 1997) argues the case for viewing Saul as a tragic hero. Preston points out that three stories are interwoven in 1 Samuel: those of Samuel, David and Saul. Any one of these three men could be the hero of the piece. But, for Preston, 'in this mirroring of lives, Saul emerges as the hero of the story' (Preston, 1997, p. 123).

Samuel could be the hero, since his birth is clearly the result of divine response to a barren woman's plea and he receives divine favour as he grows up. But he is often less than helpful to Saul, whose adviser he is and whom he betrays by anointing another man king in his place. David is chosen by God and intended for greatness, but the story reveals him to be a man of ruthless manipulation, seeking always his own good. By contrast Saul emerges as a man of integrity. Though misguided and capable of bad decisions, Saul intends to fulfil the role of leader in Israel which has fallen to his lot. He can even speak with generosity to his rival, acknowledging his own weakness, when David has spared his life (1 Sam 24:16–20). This moment of clarity foreshadows Saul's final return to his true role as military king and his heroic end at Gilboa.

The suspense is brilliantly maintained by the interposition of the story of David's revenge on the sackers of his city with the narrative of Saul's end. This interposed story

> reminds the reader that David is repairing his personal fortunes as Saul goes to his death . . . Saul dies on the battlefield, doing the job he had been appointed and elected to do – leading the army of Israel against its enemies. (Preston, 1997, p. 133)

Preston, at least, is willing to present Saul's narrative as truly tragic, reflecting both the greatness and the fatal weaknesses of a man called from obscurity to fame and authority.

By contrast, in David's case, C. Exum is less sure that there is an example of heroic tragedy. Exum acknowledges David's sufferings in scenes such as the flight from Jerusalem described above. But is the tale, as a whole, tragic? In the first part of his story David is portrayed as a pragmatic figure, someone of mundane capacity who bends with events, turning them to his own advantage. For instance, when Bathsheba's first child dies David abandons mourning since that has not turned God's will away from the child's death. Grief is no longer of practical use, so it stops. This style of presentation, Exum suggests, is weaker than that used for the presentation of the tragic career of Saul. Whereas the narrator frequently revealed Saul's inner turmoil to the reader, very little is conveyed concerning David's inner feelings in the story of his rise to power:

> Though he suffers, David is not dignified by suffering, as is Saul . . . Saul is a towering figure, not just head and shoulders above the people in stature but also in intensity . . . David, by contrast, seems small. He displays none of Saul's heroic defiance, and little, if any, of his inner struggle. (Exum, 1992, p. 142)

When disaster strikes David's children he makes no personal response. A sick child dies and death is accepted. His daughter is raped but the king takes no action. Absalom's revenge on Amnon for the rape leaves David angry but once again passive. These reactions make the king an inaccessible character whose true inner purposes the reader cannot work out. But inability to control his house leads also to David's doom; his house, his son Absalom, catches him out. It can hardly be said that David was caught out by fate unexpectedly, here, in a truly tragic manner. But David's response to Absalom's campaign touches on the tragic in his acceptance of fate, and his reaction to the murder of Absalom later in the story reveals his depth of attachment to his son and his present loss. But, even then, David returns to the daily round of his duties:

> David never wrestles, like Saul, to wrench meaning out of his misfortunes, and though he never seems quite to recover from them, he manages with the help of Joab and others, to continue with the business of kingship. (Exum, 1992, p. 148)

It is certainly true to say that the stories of both kings are presented to the reader as tragic narratives in the sense that they move from success to loss. The narratives of 1 and 2 Samuel portray the sufferings of the two kings in dramatic scenes which explore the tragedies of human life, thus highlighting these men as tragic heroes of the overall story of the struggle for the control of Israel. Saul's loss is greater than that of David and extends also to his sons. David does, ultimately, hang on to power, though at a high cost.

Tragedy as history

The stories of Saul and David are contained within a series of books which modern scholars tend to read as continuous narrative. Whereas the Hebrew Bible labels these texts the Former Prophets, modern scholars speak of a Deuteronomistic *History*. By history, here, is meant a serious enquiry into the past which leads to historiography, a written account of past events. At the level of literary criticism, then, what is encountered is historical literature. In this literary style the writer looks back at the overarching patterns of cause and effect, governing events over a prolonged time period. Such a perspective provides a suitable context for tragedy, since the historian can focus on the final end of kings and nations, the fall of civilizations, rather than on their rise and initial promise. It may also be possible to isolate chains of cause and effect where the actions, sometimes destructive actions, of one generation, cause a chain of reactions in which a descendant may suffer for the deeds of an ancestor.

In Greek literature this historical overview involves the theme of hubris and nemesis. 'Hubris' is a term for the ambition and self-satisfaction which human beings display in their attempts to dominate world events; 'Nemesis' is the term which defines the fate which awaits them, namely a catastrophe which reveals how illusory the appearance of human strength is. Hubris and nemesis are paired terms which create a cycle of rise and fall in human affairs. The pivot of this motion is the action of the gods. Hubris offends the gods, since it implies a closing of the gap between gods and human beings. Nemesis is the manner in which the gods reclaim their transcendence, putting human beings into their place by reminding them of mortality and its limitations.

One major historian of the ancient world whose work has a tragic dimension, concerning the rise and fall of great kings, is the Greek writer Herodotus. His *Histories* recounts the struggle

between the Greeks and the Persians in the sixth to fifth centuries
BCE, setting their battles for supremacy in the context of a conflict
of cultures between the despotic east and the free city state of the
west. Within this broad framework Herodotus recounts the careers
of great rulers – Candaules, Croesus and Xerxes, for example –
who rose to great power, wealth and status only to be overtaken
by disaster and sometimes by death. The manner in which catastrophe occurred to each ruler reflects the curtailment of their
ambitious pride by circumstances beyond their control. Candaules' pride in his wife's beauty, for instance, led him to shame her
and himself by encouraging another male to gaze upon her naked
body. His wife's response to this dishonour – that either the
watcher or her husband must die, led directly to Candaules' death.
(Herodotus, *Histories*, Book 1).

A recent book by F. A. J. Nielsen, *The Tragedy in History*
(1997), has compared the tragic elements to be found in Herodotus' work with those in the Deuteronomistic Histories and has
suggested five points of overall comparison between the two
histories. Both stress

- the immense distance between god and men
- that man should keep to his proper place in relationship to the
  deity
- that the activity of the deity is often deceptive
- that there is a working out of equilibrium in human affairs
  (Hubris//Nemesis)
- that people are blessed or cursed by the deity on account of
  their lineage (Nielsen, 1997, pp. 114–17).

Herodotus works out these themes in the history of the Greeks
and the Persians, showing how they operate to create tragic
situations in human affairs whereas the Deuteronomistic books
work them out across the history of Israel, the story of which is, in
its totality, a tragic work.

The Deuteronomistic Histories as tragedy

To argue for the whole Deuteronomistic history as a tragic narrative involves reading the text as an account of two main characters,
God and Israel (a whole people). From the beginnings of settlement in a Promised Land in Joshua to the loss of that Land in 2
Kings the narrative reflects on the fatal flaws which affect Israel
and lead to its inevitable doom and destruction.

This manner of treating tragedy is in contrast to Steiner's view that the Bible cannot hit the right note of unexpected and irrational catastrophe since God, a major figure in the text, is a being whose purposes are known. The presentation of catastrophe as punishment on sin removes, for Steiner, the open-ended nature of tragic events in classical literature such as the *Iliad*.

> The fall of . . . Jerusalem is merely just, where the fall of Troy is the first great metaphor of tragedy. Where a city is destroyed because it has defied God, its destruction is a passing instant in the rational design of God's purpose. (Steiner, 1961, p. 5)

Even in the Deuteronomistic books, however, the entire meaning of the narrative is not summed up in the simple message of retribution. God, acting as providence, continually offers Israel a blessing, but Israel's own actions bring about her defeat, as much as do divine pronouncements of wrath. Moreover the moral dimension of this stage setting – the way in which the characters take responsibility for their actions and the consequences of these acts – operates as a motif in classical tragedy and in Shakespearian tragedy, as well as in biblical tragic stories.

Israel's character

Israel's character is composed both of greatness and of flaws. The greatness comes from the promises made by God to the fledgling nation. Freed from slavery through divine intervention (the Exodus) and led through the desert by a divinely-appointed leader (Moses) the people arrive in a fruitful land which they are promised will be their long-term home. But Israel's human response is ambivalent. There are great leaders such as Moses and Joshua who bring the people close to God, but there are also bad interludes between leaders when the people fall away from their patron deity.

At the same time not all Israel's leaders are without flaw. Saul and David each have their own weaknesses and encounter divine hostility, as shown earlier in this chapter. In the later Deuteronomistic books some kings are basically bad, such as Jeroboam with his institution of an alternative cult in the north (1 Kgs 12) and the last kings of Judah in the south, after the time of Manasseh (2 Kgs 21). Israel, then, has a history composed of greatness impaired by fatal flaws on the part of the people, a combination which leads inexorably downwards to the Exile. This overarching treatment gives support to the argument that this is tragic literature.

From generation to generation

One of the subthemes which creates the link across all stages of Israelite history in these books is the manner in which what one generation does affects later generations. Nielsen remarks on the chain of events in Herodotus, in relation to the struggles between Greeks and Persians:

When Candaules became infatuated by the beauty of his wife, a chain of historical events was started that was to continue for several hundred years and to culminate in the ignominious defeat of the Persians. (Nielsen, 1997, p. 79)

C. Exum applies this theme to the Israelite history of the Deuteronomistic books in her investigation of the fate of the members of Saul's house. The story of Saul's descendants is interwoven with the story of Saul and David. The guilt for Saul's crimes is visited on his descendants, while David carries the bloodguilt for the death of the Saulides. 2 Samuel 21:1–14 brings to a close the chain of tragic events which had beset the house of Saul. Seven of Saul's descendants are brutally sacrificed to God as atonement for crimes committed in the past against the Gibeonites. The tragedy of this episode 'derives from the shocking events, events that evoke a sense of outrage at the unremitting demands of destiny and the deity against Saul's house' (Exum, 1992, p. 110). The tale of bloodguilt and atonement, of divine displeasure and appeasement has echoes of Greek tragedies where the actions of one generation trigger reactions for many years to come.

Israel: a guilty people?

As well as the theme of generational guilt carried across the generations in royal houses, the Deuteronomistic histories contain the theme of the guilt of the whole nation in all its generations. Nielsen refers to this theme when he treats the guilt of the divided monarchy in two separate 'characters', Israel and Judah (Nielsen, 1997, pp. 143–51). Each character involves a chain of generations which in their fullness make up the character, and in each case there is the same starting point, the fact that each kingdom traces its existence to the one God, YHWH, and so owes allegiance to that deity:

Yahweh is a jealous and passionate god who will not forgive Israel's transgressions and sins . . . The Israelites are given a choice and they seal their own fate by that choice. (Nielsen, 1997, p. 121)

Blessing and cursing are the elements of tragedy, for blessing implies hope for future development while cursing implies destruction. When Jeroboam takes over the kingship of the north and establishes a cult of two bull-calves the doom of Israel is foreshadowed (Nielson, 1997, p. 143). Thus tragedy embraces both leader and nation in a single narrative of human choice and divine retribution.

Likewise with Judah there is an overarching tragic narrative which continues from Solomon to the last Davidic king. Though Judah inherits divine promises of support given to the ancestor, David (2 Sam 7), Judah suffers under the same jealous divine control as does Israel. Hezekiah and Josiah stand out as good men who try to reform their people's understanding and so prevent disaster, but their efforts are less significant, in the end, than the succession of kings who trust in their human designs and so lead the people astray (Nielsen, 1997, p. 154).

Israel: a tragic people?

Neilsen asks 'If the Deuteronomistic history is a tragedy, then who is the tragic hero?' and answers 'I would suggest that the people of Israel should be regarded as the tragic hero of the Deuteronomistic history' (Nielsen, 1997, p. 154). For the Deuteronomistic History, 'being the history of the Jewish people, does not contain a single, overriding, tragic hero. Instead the people might be regarded as such a hero' (Nielsen, 1997, p. 155).

Ultimately the tragedy of Israel is the fact that the people cannot live out their potential greatness, falling back from initial promise. Within the macrocosm of Israel the careers of Saul and David provide microcosms of this pattern. Each ruler's story exhibits the same pattern of initial hope for successful rule distorted by human ambition and passionate desires. The tragic mode can be said to dominate since the end of each story is one of gloom. In the case of Israel as a whole that gloom is reflected on a massive scale which is prophesied by Moses in Deuteronomy 28:65–66.

8

Reading stories, finding women

From national issues of hubris and nemesis this book now turns to the role of women in the Deuteronomistic narratives. In the previous chapter attention focused on the great male figures of Israel's past such as Saul and David. The stories of Saul and David are easily remembered, since the Deuteronomistic texts tell their story from the viewpoint of the great public events of the history of Israel, whereas women in the Deuteronomistic narratives generally take a minor role and their careers are often used as tools for revealing the character of the male figure on whom the narrative centres.

Are women, then, of no concern for the reader of the books Joshua to 2 Kings? It is certainly the case that a number of women characters are present in the Deuteronomistic books and that, in some cases, a good deal of information about them is available. However they tend to be known as 'Wife of X' or 'Daughter of Y'. Thus Bathsheba first appears as wife of Uriah and then as David's woman, someone who is disposed of by males, while Jephthah's daughter is not even given a personal name. Women, on first reading, operate in the background of the narratives; focusing on women means turning the text around in order to put them in the foreground.

There is a further issue to be investigated in the process of turning narratives around to find women in their own right – that is, the frequently implied criticism of women in the text. Women who do take centre stage are often negatively assessed. Thus Delilah is shown in a bad light, as the seducer of the great Israelite hero, Samson. Samson is weak because he falls for Delilah's charms but she is an evil woman who betrays her lover to his enemies. Later, in the books of Kings, Jezebel is also negatively assessed for her takeover of her husband's royal authority.

These negative assessments of women are not unusual or

isolated aspects of the text, but form part of an overall critique of social roles carried out by the writers of the Deuteronomistic works. The social system which holds this view of women is described by scholars as 'patriarchy'. This term defines societies where men dominate and where they control the lives of women; such societies were many in the ancient world, including ancient Israel. The Deuteronomistic texts mirror the social values of the society which produced them.

Postmodernity and women

But twentieth century Western society is no longer dominated by such an approach to women. Men and women are viewed equally as full human beings and as free citizens. Thus women now have a legal status equal to that of men and can control their own property, while also contributing to the political scene. This social change has had an impact on how the Bible is read, by female readers especially. Women with an interest in the meaning of biblical texts look for a message relevant to their contemporary life-experience and do not necessarily find the older reading of the text, which accepted patriarchal bias, acceptable.

Women readers have explored the possibilities of a new style of exegesis and have seriously critiqued the idea that the Bible is good for women. These developments have led to the rise of feminist criticism, as a school of thought. Not that there is any one style of interpretation common to all feminist interpretations of the Bible; rather the term 'feminist criticism' is a broad term which incorporates a variety of individual exegetical methods.

Women and *The Post Modern Bible*

In the book *The Post Modern Bible*, one chapter is devoted to feminist and womanist criticism. The intention is to lay bare agendas connected to gender and power relationships through

> readings that demonstrate how texts construct readers by imposing ideologies of gender and power and how readers can resist those constructions through a critical engagement with *feminism* and *womanism*. (Bible Collective, 1995, p. 225)

One part of this task is to name the women whose stories occur in the Bible as persons in their own right, that is, to retrieve the images of women from the text. A further stage is to engage with the overall ideology, its nature and consequences.

E. Schüssler Fiorenza has been working at this task over many years. For her patriarchy is ultimately about social oppression. It is a way of thinking which endorses oppression of marginal social groups by dominant ones; feminist criticism here turns into a form of liberationism (Bible Collective, 1995, p. 261). For Schüssler Fiorenza the purpose of feminist critique must be to alert the reader to the way in which a biblical book encourages her or him to accept the inevitability of unequal power relations in society, through its rhetorical structure. The reader of Jezebel's story, for example, is encouraged to gaze with acceptance as Jezebel's dead body is attacked by the street dogs. This fate, it is implied, is the result of the woman's usurpation of the male role – as well as the punishment for indirect murder.

Mieke Bal, another notable feminist critic, operates as a narratologist, situating her work at the intersection of feminism and literary theory (Bible Collective, 1995, p. 255). Bal avoids looking for one, absolutely valid, interpretation of text. Instead she highlights the variety of meanings a reader may take from a book, by using narrative criticism, language theory or psychoanalysis. This in turn creates in the reader an acceptance of variety, which allows different interpretations equal validity.

Schüssler Fiorenza and Bal are examples of very different possibilities for reading text which have emerged from the contemporary focus on women in their own right. Each in her own way requires the student of the Bible to be a self-conscious reader, aware both of their own act of reading and of the way in which the text itself operates. Where a reader identifies the persuasion of the text towards agreeing with unequal social or political structures, she or he must resist the text's influence, so 'reading against the grain' of the book.

Narrative and reading against the grain

Because the Deuteronomistic Histories are inherently narrative in style, there is always a narrator present in the text, the voice that tells the story to the reader. The narrator is a major influence on the reader's interpretation of the meaning of the events being narrated, even though the narrator is an anonymous figure. Reading against the grain entails becoming more aware of the narrator as a force to be reckoned with, and may require a resistance to the values held by the narrator, shown in the judgements passed on persons and events.

A. Bach has explored the reader's response to a narrator in

chapter two of *Women, Seduction and Betrayal in Biblical Narrative* (1997). She begins by defining the importance of the narrative voice:

> Because the Bible is a text that has occupied a central place in the unconscious of western culture, its characters survive in the minds of readers. The biblical narrator can be considered as one of those voices who live on in the mind. (Bach, 1997, p. 13)

Bach urges that one should not go along with the narrator in blind obedience but should shift

> readerly identity from that of ideal reader, an individual who would believe, understand and appreciate every word and device of the text, to that of suspicious narratee (i.e., recipient of narrator's message). (Bach, 1997, p. 15)

Bach points out that the narrator in biblical texts often stands in the place of the deity, describing God's reactions to human actions and revealing God's purpose to the reader. If the narrator speaks from a male perspective, then the male view of society is aligned with the view of it held by an omniscient divine being. This male view, inscribed in the text, is portrayed as the correct reading of events which should be adopted by the reader. The effect is to reinforce a male-dominant perspective on social roles and values.

With relation to women in the Deuteronomistic books, the male view evidences an ambivalent evaluation of woman. On the one hand the Strange Woman, the woman outside the family circle, is viewed as seducer. 'She pulls men inside her, into a place of darkness and chaos, like Lilith or Delilah' (Bach, 1997, p. 28). On the other hand, a good wife who meets her husband's needs is to be valued. The young Abishag is such a wife to the elderly David, ready at table and in bed, to keep the king company, to warm and comfort him (1 Kgs 1). It may, then, be necessary to resist the narrator who wishes the reader to boo Delilah and applaud Abishag (Bach, 1997, p. 26).

In this context Bach suggests that a narrative has its own life; shorn of its narrator it can be reread and reinterpreted by the reader who gives it a different emphasis. In the story of David, for instance, the women who are linked with the king are dealt with in separate scenes. Abigail, Michal and Bathsheba never share dialogue with one another. This keeping apart is one means by which the narrator controls the influence of these characters on the reader. But since all three women are contemporaneous, all three are wives to David the king, it would be possible to imagine them as interactive. Reading and interpreting the narrative in this way allows women's values to be heard. 'Abigail and Michal do not keen for Bathsheba's dead baby son. But in my mind they do' (Bach, 1997, p. 27).

Reading stories

Feminist criticism provides the rudiments of a new reading style for the Deuteronomistic works. At base, this is a narratological style which involves reading the text carefully with regard to character, plot, narrator and language. An extra dimension is the need to put women characters in the foreground and to explore carefully plots which involve women, all the time resisting a male narrator's interpretation of these elements of the story.

It is not a question of reading a story in order to find the truth of the original event, but rather to establish the impact which the story makes on the reader. This in turn entails a conscious deliberation about the nature of the reader's own preconceptions and how these lead the reader to receive the text and make it their own. As C. Exum states, in *Plotted, Shot and Painted* (1996):

> The twin focus [is] on representation – the way women are portrayed in biblical narratives and both the social assumptions and unconscious motivations that create such portrayals – and interpretation – the way we explain the meaning of these narratives in the light of our own attitudes and circumstances. (Exum, 1996, p. 9)

Finding women

It is now possible to turn to the stories of two women from the Deuteronomistic Histories – Delilah and Bathsheba – and to examine them in detail from a feminist perspective. Delilah is actually part of the story of Samson while Bathsheba is part of David's story. Both women play significant roles in the events depicted in the Deuteronomistic history of Israel – Delilah being responsible for Israelite collapse and Bathsheba being the mother of the great king, Solomon. To describe them thus is to view them from the male perspective which deplores the collapse of Samson and remembers the name of the king's mother. But there is enough material in each story for a reader to consider the women as characters in their own right.

Judges 16

Delilah appears in the middle of the story of the folk hero Samson. Samson has already taken several women to him as concubines and now he 'loved a woman in the valley of Sorek, whose name was Delilah' (Judg 16:4). Delilah is then persuaded by the Philistine leaders to help them defeat Samson, the reward being a small fortune. Samson has a secret source of power, his uncut hair. In a series of repetitious scenes Delilah begs Samson to tell her his secret. Each time he names a different source, but each time his power remains intact and he breaks the cords with which he is bound. Finally Delilah reproaches Samson with his lack of love in refusing to tell her his secret and he is persuaded. While Samson sleeps in Delilah's lap the hair is cut and the Philistines drag him away as a captive.

The narrator passes no overt judgement on Delilah, but he tells the story in a manner which emphasizes her deceitfulness. She is not honourable and cannot resist a bribe. She plays on the poor man's infatuation with her. Finally she betrays him and turns him over into captivity. A Laffey points out in *Wives, Harlots and Concubines* (1988) that patriarchal bias is at work here. What does the phrase 'Samson loved . . .' mean, for instance?

> She may . . . have been the victim of lust. If he had taken advantage of her, then, given the patriarchal culture, she was in no position to send him away. There is no mention of marriage. (Laffey, 1988, p. 104)

Delilah is not exactly deceitful since she asks openly for the information she wants, and includes hints that she wants to know how to bind and subdue him. Samson could have understood her real meaning and prevented his own downfall. Also, since Sorek is the name of a non-Israelite site, Delilah may not even have been an Israelite. Thus she may not have been a traitor to her own people. Laffey denies the validity, then, of labelling Delilah as the archetypal temptress.

C. Exum comments on this use of Delilah as a cultural symbol for temptation and deceit: 'As a cultural symbol, what she represents is rivalled perhaps only by two other biblical figures, whose names, like hers, have passed into popular usage: Jezebel . . . and . . . Judas' (Exum, 1996, p. 176). But what justification does the text of Judges have for this view? Delilah remains a somewhat vague figure in terms of parentage and social standing. She appears as an independent woman since she is not identified in relation to father or husband in the manner of most Deuteronomistic women of good standing. But it is not stated that she is a whore. The lack of details allows the reader to supply them from his or her own preconceptions: 'In particular, the process that results in typecasting Delilah as a Philistine prostitute can be understood as what happens when readers automatically adopt the view of women encoded in the story' (Exum, 1996, p. 186).

Exum suggests that Delilah is presented by the narrator of Judges as a Bad Woman, a type balanced by the Other Woman in Samson's story, his mother, who carries out, as wife and mother, 'the two valued roles for a woman in ancient Israelite society, and knows her place' (Exum, 1996, p. 186).

Delilah provides a moral dimension for Samson's story, but this is a moral message based on male values and offered from a male perspective in which women are defined as a temptation and a snare (Exum, 1996, p. 188). Yet Laffey's comment, referred to above, offers an alternative evaluation of Delilah as illustrating what courses of action may be open to a woman on her own in society, caught between the pressures from the different males who surround her.

2 Samuel 11

The first part of Bathsheba's story occurs when David has gained control of Israel and is securely established as king. She is the object of the king's attentions. Instead of going on campaign he relaxes at home where he sees her having a ritual bath. He sends for her and beds her. She conceives and sends him a blunt message 'I am with child' (verse 5). The rest of this scenario focuses on David's attempts to pass the child off as Uriah's by encouraging the man to sleep with his wife and, when he fails to persuade Uriah to visit his home, on his responsibility for Uriah's death in battle, engineered so that no public scandal can touch the king. Bathsheba has no part in this until the death of Uriah when 'she made lamentation for her husband' (verse 26). But she is still under David's control and he takes her to his house as his wife.

Once again the text focuses on David, who is judged by God and told that the child to be born will die because of David's sin. Bathsheba finally appears again – this time in mourning for her child. But even here the stress is on the king's male role: 'David comforted his wife . . . and lay with her; and she bore a son, and he called his name Solomon' (2 Sam 12:24). C. Exum comments on the androcentric narration of Bathsheba's story:

> The point is we are not allowed access to her point of view . . . by
> portraying Bathsheba in an ambiguous light, the narrator leaves her
> vulnerable, not simply to assault by David but also to misappropria-
> tion by those who . . . offer their versions of . . . the story. (Exum,
> 1996, pp. 22–3)

Some commentators on the text of 2 Samuel have wanted to
blame Bathsheba for what happened. By letting herself be seen
bathing in the open, was the woman not inviting male attention?
Exum objects: 'What about the responsibility of the narrator, who
made the decision to portray her in the act of washing? It is, after
all, the biblical narrator who . . . makes Bathsheba the object of
the male gaze' (Exum, 1996, p. 25).

A. Bach, writing on the same scene, states that 'In a narration
that reveals nothing of the woman's response to the king, her
silence reinforces the power relationship between the king and the
woman brought to his bed' (Bach, 1997, p. 161). Bach parts
company with the narrator to reimagine the scene between Bathsheba and David. Using the parallel story of Amnon's rape of
Tamar, she imagines the words which Tamar uses in that scene to
prevent violence being done to her on the lips of Bathsheba as she
faces David. Thus Bathsheba ceases to be a silent character and
has a voice with which to contribute to the discussion of her own
future. In this situation, far from being a temptress, Bathsheba
emerges as a woman wronged by the male power structures of her
context.

I Kings 1

Part two of Bathsheba's story occurs in 1 Kings. Here David is an
old man and Bathsheba the mother of the future king. 'Speaking
in the familiar cadences of a deferential wife, she is no longer
dangerous . . . Bathsheba now plays an acceptable social role'
(Bach, 1997, p. 162). She urges David to confirm her son as king,
an act which will fulfill the divine promise of 2 Samuel 7. Although
Bathsheba appears here as a woman at home in her setting, able
to tackle the king, she is still, nevertheless, under male control
since it is Nathan who has suggested to her that she should
approach David on Solomon's behalf. Bathsheba's subordination
to the men in her life is made clear: 'Then Bathsheba bowed with
her face to the ground, and did obeisance to the king' (verse 31).

Bathsheba's political role is one limited and shaped by male
desires and male rivalry insofar as her words and actions are

controlled by the narrative framework established by the narrator. In order to set her centre stage it is necessary to remove Bathsheba from the narrator's control, to set her free from the text so that her character can be independently developed.

Women in Judges

The narrative control of women's stories is to be found not only in individual stories but in whole books. The book of Judges, for instance, contains a great many women's stories, yet these are controlled by the narrative force of the book. The book of Judges is about the settlement of the land by Israel and the wars Israel fought to hold onto its territory. Male Israelites feature in this narrative context as warriors and military chieftains. In this male context the characterization of the women serves the overall male interests of the text. Deborah and Jael are great women because they save the people in times of conflict. They temporarily become 'male', having male virtues of determination, courage, mental and physical endurance. The urgency of the danger endorses their acting outside female roles and their courage shames the men of Israel who have not acted so well in Israel's behalf. In the story of Jephthah his daughter's conduct provides a model of extreme commitment to the public interest. She accepts the sacrifice of her own life in return for Israel's martial success, even though she knew nothing of her father's vow and had no part in it.

These are portraits of honourable women, women who are models of male values. They are partnered, in Judges, by two other models, that of the woman as seducer in Delilah and that of woman as object of male abuse in the Levite's wife who was gang-raped, left for dead and whose dismembered body was sent, by her husband, throughout Israel (Judg 19). In these last two models of woman the underlying commentary in the narrative is on women's sexuality and women's bodies. The Levite's woman bears the penalty for all women whose sexuality is so dangerous to men that it must always be controlled. Exum comments, in *Judges and Method* (in Yee (ed.), 1995):

> Because it has offended the woman's sexuality must be destroyed and its threat diffused by scattering. Cutting up the woman can be viewed on a psychological level . . . as an expression of male fear of women's sexuality. (Exum, 1995, p. 84)

Horrible as the story of the concubine is, it may have some mitigating circumstances. When the pieces of the body reach the people they are shocked and comment that nothing like this has ever happened before. It may be that here the narrator himself hesitates to applaud male abuse of women. The woman's death triggers further bloody reprisals so that society appears to degenerate into brutal aggression. The terrible fate of the Levite's wife illustrates the brutality of which men are capable and which is to be deplored. In this setting the concubine is a victim whose fate rouses the people to some awareness of their degenerating society. As Jephthah's daughter was a sacrificial victim for victory, so the concubine is a victim to open the people's eyes to disaster.

Women, strange and good

In the OT male values, inscribed in the text, tend to relegate women to two categories, the Strange Woman and the Good Woman. The Strange Woman is strange because she is an outsider. Like Delilah, she is not attached to any male protecting figure in society and so her behaviour is not socially monitored. The Strange Woman is synonymous with Temptress. This identification turns on women's sexual role. Normally a woman uses her sexuality under male control, as a virgin daughter, bringing a good price to her father, or as a wife and mother of a man's sons. But the Strange Woman stands outside these relationships and so can use her own sexuality as she wishes. This make her a danger to men, for she will seek lovers by seducing men to their disadvantage. This model has been discussed above with regard to the stories of Delilah and Bathsheba.

By contrast, the Good Woman is safely under the authority of her menfolk. She speaks and acts in the text within this social framework, as does the older Bathsheba when she sought audience with her husband and bowed low before him on gaining her request. Young women are also slotted into this household context. Bach imagines the Bathsheba scene as including the new, young wife, Abishag. As the older women no longer catches the male gaze of the reader, the male eye wanders around the chamber and catches sight of a new interest. 'It roams over the eager Abishag, desperately trying to become the new Spectacle queen in the empire of the gaze' (Bach, 1997, p. 163).

Abishag's status depends on her attractiveness to her man. She has been put into that position by other men who have chosen her to be the king's companion. When David dies her future lies with the man who will take her; in 1 Kings it is Adonijah who attempts to do this. The young, sexually desirable woman is squabbled over by contending males, a pawn in their contest for the throne of Israel. As a Good Woman Abishag has no say of her own but submits to the men's decisions about her future.

Occasionally Strange Women can become Good Women. In Judges Jael becomes a Good Woman when she sides with Israel and kills Sisera, driving the tent peg through his head while he sleeps in her tent. When Delilah has Samson sleeping in her lap and betrays him she is a Strange Woman; when Jael has Sisera sleeping in her tent and betrays him she is a Good Woman. Both presentations are creations of the narrative voice who puts loyalty to the insider of the text, that is Israel, as a first priority. But are not Jael and Delilah sisters? As women lacking male protectors they each have to make difficult decisions about the man who has come into their home. Both women throw their lot in with what seems to be the stronger side in the war between Israel and its neighbours.

Final thoughts

It is up to the reader to decide whether to be won over by the categorization of woman into good and bad along lines which are decided by the male narrative voice. But even if the reader accepts this view of female social roles, some women's stories challenge the simple black–white evaluation. The story of the Levite's wife is one such event. Surely the degree of violence used against her makes her into a neutral symbol of injustice. Just as later in the Deuteronomistic books, in 2 Samuel 13, Amnon's refusal to listen to his half-sister's pleas for right conduct and restraint make her, too, into a symbol of all those oppressed persons whose voice is never heard in the political centre of affairs. Both women and men readers can pass, through these stories, to a broader reflection on human society and human relationships in which the distinctions of gender are temporarily lost sight of and the species, as a whole, becomes the focus of attention.

History as Theology

9

A constitution for Israel

In the first section of this book historical issues relating to Joshua to 2 Kings were examined. These issues arise from the obvious fact that the books appear to contain a history of Israel. It became clear that the material has to be treated as historiography rather than history, and this led to the topic of the literary nature of the Deuteronomistic books. The second section therefore employed the techniques of narrative criticism to explore the meanings of the text. It was clear in both sections, however, that the Deuteronomistic texts are religious books whose purpose is to convey theological ideas about the relationship betwen the God of Israel and his people. The third section of this book turns now to the question of the theological issues dealt with in the narrative of the texts from Joshua to 2 Kings.

The foundation for the religious message of the Deuteronomistic books is the political and social development of Israel, as this is depicted in the OT. There is no speculation about the inner nature of God as a philosophical topic in its own right, unrelated to human affairs. The focus of the texts is on the significance of God's existence for one particular society, Israel. The title, Deuteronomistic Histories, which holds together the account of YHWH and Israel, is derived from the book of Deuteronomy. The continuity of title across several works reflects the views of M. Noth, who thought that there was a deliberate authorial design at work in the way in which Joshua to 2 Kings follow on from the story of Deuteronomy. It is possible to suggest that this structure contains a two-part reflection on the nature of ancient Israelite society – the origins and basic principles, followed by how these worked out in ongoing historical events.

This argument can be developed further to suggest that Deuteronomy presents, in a religious context, the constitution of Israel. The law codes of Deuteronomy 12–26 set out the manner in which society is to be organized once Israel is settled in the Land. The Deuteronomistic Histories recount how far Israel, in its generations, kept to that constitution and what happened when they failed to do so. Partly then, the Deuteronomistic texts are a form of political commentary; but they are also books of theology. In Deuteronomy Moses reminds the people that it is YHWH who has chosen them to be a nation, has ensured their freedom from slavery and who will now establish them in a land of their own. YHWH continues to be a decisive actor in the playing out of Israel's subsequent life experience.

The theology of the Deuteronomistic Histories, then, concerns the ideas about God and Israel which the books put forward. It involves particular attitudes both to deity and to people as well as an investigation of the linking relationship between these two. The stories of individual heroes and of the nation as a whole are shaped by the overarching religious messages which the writers of the text wished to convey. Another term for this shaping of meaning is 'ideology'. Ideology here refers to the principles of interpretation which underlie the text and which stem from the views of the authors.

Ideological criticism

Scholars have increasingly come to realize the importance of searching out the ideological attitudes found in texts. No text is free from ideology; each story in the Deuteronomistic works, for instance, is told from a particular viewpoint expressed in the voice of the narrator. *The Post Modern Bible* states that 'ideology is to be encountered in the discourse of every text – in both what a text says and what it does not say' (Bible Collective, 1995, p. 274). The ideology of a text is linked to the cultural contexts of writers and readers. A text may endorse the political or social status quo of the writer's society. In this context ideology is connected with issues of power, since a person who reads a text and accepts its underlying ideology is led to one acceptable response to the world around.

These matters have already been raised in connection with women's stories in the Deuteronomistic Histories, in the last chapter. Feminist criticism seeks to uncover the ideology of a text (in this case, patriarchal issues) and then to reread the text avoiding an unthinking acceptance of the text's social values. Feminist reading of texts is one example of ideological criticism. Liberationist reading is another. In liberationist reading readers 'find themselves constantly pushing against the boundaries of the text, asking questions that challenge the given social order by questioning its myths, values . . . and practices' (Bible Collective, 1995, p. 281).

A liberationist reading of Joshua will avoid aligning the reader with the dominant politics of the book, in which Israel's interests come first and the interests of the Canaanites a poor second. Rather the reader will be encouraged to examine the manner in which Joshua deals with cultures and social groups which are marginal to the concerns of the Israelites.

Ideological criticism thus seeks to operate against dominant political and social tendencies in a text. It is to this degree an ethical activity, requiring the reader to examine the morality of particular interpretations of texts and of certain messages about where absolute authority lies:

> Ideological criticism . . . has to do with the ethical character of and response to, the text . . . when it comes to reading biblical texts . . . and making sense of the ideological discourse, struggles and conflicts of the Bible, the reader is faced with the challenge of and responsibility for, ethical questioning . . . (Bible Collective, 1995, p. 275)

In the context of the OT, ideological criticism involves the disentangling of several strands of meaning. There is the strand associated with the absolute authority of a divine being. Then there is the strand associated with those who wrote the biblical texts. These texts were preserved by the leaders of communities both Jewish and Christian, having been produced by Israelite/Jewish writers for the elite classes of their day. Although the books refer to people and nation as a whole, it is usually the upper classes whose interests are served in the texts. The Ten Commandments, for instance, appear to describe basic ethical behaviour for all citizens; but whose interests do the commandments relate to? Surely they relate to those who have property and family and a good social status. In the ancient world such persons would be the elite classes, rather than slaves or tied labourers. In this context the OT deals with political theology. It weaves together the political interests of dominant social groups with a particular attitude towards the nature and concerns of the patron deity.

A further issue is that of the values held by readers of the text. The Deuteronomistic works offer evaluations of Israelite society to the reader who must decide whether these evaluations are appropriate or not. Each reader brings to the task of reading his or her own preconceived ideas about God and society. A reader who associates with the term 'Israel' will read the story of Israel's partial failure to take control of Canaan with regret. Israel did not have enough faith in God to deny existence to foreign cultures and their beliefs. But a reader who associates with the concept of Canaan will read the same story with mixed feelings: relief that Israel did not exterminate Canaanites and anger that the rights of Canaanites were so ignored in the first place.

These comments indicate how complex an issue ideological criticism is, and how careful the reader must be in sorting out the layers of meaning in a book when operating from an ideological-critical perspective. This has implications also for the term 'theology'. The theology of the Deuteronomistic texts is a form of ideology. Although the text often narrates the story of Israel as from the divine viewpoint, this is a reflection of what the writers and their society thought God intended. It is not a question of falsehood here. Writers honestly and sincerely portray the religious beliefs of their contemporary society. But, from a critical perspective, it has to be admitted that the texts reflect God mediated through a human lens. As human societies change, so do the values held by writers and readers. The vexed question of the invasion of Canaan by Israel is one example where modern readers may not begin from the same system of social belief as did ancient readers.

It is appropriate, then, to examine theological interpretation of textual meaning in its own right as a matter for critical evaluation. 'The theology of the Deuteronomistic Histories' is not something to be taken on board without first considering carefully the issues it raises.

Old Testament theology

Another issue which needs to be addressed emerges from the phrase 'OT theology'. This phrase implies that there is one OT and one overarching theology to be found equally in all its parts. However, scholarship has shown that the OT is a library, a collection of diverse material from different sources, which has been gathered together over time. Not all this material has the same interests. Whereas Deuteronomy focuses on Israelite traditions to do with YHWH, with the themes of Exodus and Land, the wisdom books speak more often of success or failure in the life of an individual and refer to the deity by the common ancient Near Eastern title God (El) rather than by the personal name of Israel's deity.

If the books are diverse so also are the themes which can be extracted from them. Scholars such as W. Eichrodt and G. Von Rad believed that it was possible to take themes such as Covenant and to show how the entire OT was a treatment of those particular themes. With regard to the topic of Covenant, this may work well as a base for exploring the contents of Torah and Prophecy where a number of covenant forms are found in the divine pacts with Noah, Abraham, Moses and David. But the term 'covenant' is not one found in the wisdom books overall nor in some of the other short texts within the Writings. Even with Torah and Prophecy it is possible to over-harmonize the covenantal material, treating them all as the same reality, when in fact the content of the several agreements are quite separate – Abraham is promised a son, for instance, while Moses represents Israel in a national treaty with YHWH. If the field is narrowed to the Mosaic Covenant it is true that material relating to this can be found in four of the five books of Law and in works such as Jeremiah and Ezekiel. But that is still some way from proving that one single strand of theology was intentionally developed in a systematic way across the entire OT.

The development of modern methods of biblical criticism has also affected the way in which scholars view texts. Source critics argued that behind existing whole texts lie stages of text development when smaller versions were expanded and short texts originally separate were run together. Form critics pointed to the way in which passages were built up from a number of tiny individual elements – a proverb, or a short story, or an oracle. The task of composition may have been more like that of editing, leaving little room for a single theological theme to give rise to co-ordinated treatments by a single author. All of this means that any account of the message of the OT has to be handled under the title of 'theologies' rather than that of 'theology'.

W. Brueggemann is one scholar who has exerted himself to bring together the results of modern critical scholarship with the ongoing desire of scholars to produce systematic accounts of biblical theology. While respecting the individual value of particular books he has also explored underlying beliefs about God carried by the texts. In *Old Testament Theology* (1992), he argues that 'the Old Testament is a collage of documents that bring to speech what seems to be going on in Israel's strange linkage with Yahweh' (Brueggemann, 1992, p. 23). He works with a two-part concept, that of hurt and hope. He points out the tendency of OT texts to establish a blueprint for relationships between God and human beings as is evident in Genesis 1–2 where God is a being who establishes a pattern of ordered relationship between creation and himself and between the different species of creatures and between creatures and habitat. The idea of a fixed order to creation is mirrored in an unchanging social system, such as is often found connected with the institution of monarchy. But this model of order is in tension with the Exodus model. Pharaoh can be viewed as a clear example of a *status quo* leader whose rule is oppressively rigid. In Exodus 1 the Israelites cry out in their hurt under Pharaoh's servants and God hears. In the Exodus motif oppressive, fixed political order is broken apart by divine intervention. From this emerges hope, hope for a new social and political order which will offer a better theological paradigm:

> The entrance of pain is a *crucial minority voice* in the Old Testament that peculiarly characterises both the God of Israel and the people of Israel . . . It is this embrace of pain that opens the Old Testament to the future . . . (Brueggemann, 1992, p. 26)

In this framework Deuteronomy stands as a bridge between hurt and hope. Deuteronomy is presented as a social future not yet in operation (Brueggemann, 1992, p. 80). Brueggemann's approach here is a form of OT theology which attempts to extract basic principles from actual texts while also being sensitive to the individual content of the member texts of the OT library.

The Deuteronomistic style

Picking up on both linkages and distinctions between books in the OT it is possible to focus on the Deuteronomistic texts as a sub-collection within the Hebrew Scriptures. Clearly Deuteronomy is a different book from the Histories but, then, each of the Histories has its own specific content. Yet there are certain modes of thought which are particular to these texts. R. Mason, in *Propaganda and Subversion in the Old Testament* (1997), addresses the distinctive general features of Deuteronomistic thought. He picks out the theme of land and conquest as the propaganda face of the material. God in Deuteronomy makes a promise of a land gift to Israel and lays out the manner in which this gift will be obtained, namely by a violent invasion of a territory already populated by other nations. Although archaeological evidence shows that such a conquest did not take place, nonetheless the propaganda value of the text remains a potential influence on the reader.

Mason argues that the vocabulary of a land gained in difficult circumstances, in the face of great hostility, and held with the

support of a patron deity was part of normal ancient Near Eastern
ideology and Deuteronomy should be evaluated within that context; its ongoing power for endorsing violence occurs when the
Deuteronomistic perspective is separated from its original life
setting (Mason, 1997, p. 75). Although the propaganda of holy
war found in the Deuteronomistic texts endorses the validity of
Israel as a political formation, there are other aspects of Deuteronomistic thought which run counter to this tendency. Mason
reflects on the subversion of the institution of monarchy found in
Deuteronomy and the Deuteronomistic Histories.

In Deuteronomy the role of a king is accepted but also controlled. The king is more like a philosopher than an absolute
authority in the land (Deut 17:14-20). At the same time the
Deuteronomistic Histories cast doubt on the value of a king in 1
Samuel 11. Here the dialogue between Samuel and God indicates
that the author of the book thought of God as the only true ruler
of Israel and regarded human kingship as a poor substitute for
theocratic rule. Although God also makes promises to kings, as in
the promise of longterm support of the Davidic line of kings in 2
Samuel 7, and David is presented in the books of Samuel as
favoured by the God of Israel, kings are ultimately responsible for
the downfall of Judah and Israel and are the major source of the
weakness of Israel's response to God's commands, both religious
and social (Mason, 1997, p. 79). Deuteronomistic style attacks
the oppressive reality of established systems of power and the
ambivalent nature of absolute authority vested in institutions, in
ancient Israel especially, but, implicitly, wherever such systems
occur (Mason, 1997, p. 85).

Mason concentrates on propaganda and subversion as perspectives from which to approach OT text. G. McConville and J. G.
Millar choose rather the themes of time and place as tools for
interpreting Deuteronomic thought:

> The prologue to ... [Deuteronomy] presents two fundamental
> concepts. The first is that Israel is a nation on the move – engaged
> on a journey with Yahweh ... The second concept cannot be
> separated from the first, since it asserts that the past experience of
> Israel holds the key to enjoyment of their covenant relationship.
> (McConville and Millar, 1994, p. 31)

Thus time and place are two parts of Israel's relationship with its
God. Time involves both movement and set timeframes. Looking
at the Deuteronomistic texts as a whole, Israel is always moving
through time; yet time stands still for a while when Israel meets

YHWH at Mt Horeb and in Moab. Israel is the product both of time past and of a moving timeframe (McConville and Millar, 1994, p. 44). Time is woven with the theme of place. Each decision to obey God which the Israelites make is at a certain place – an idea which points forward to the final place for Israel, that is, the land in which they are to stay for their generations and where they are to keep the detailed law codes set out in Deuteronomy 12–26. The twin themes of time and place, then, contain 'the key Deuteronomic tension between the transcendence and the immanence of God' (McConville and Millar, 1994, p. 36). For the Deuteronomist God is both beyond human comprehension and also, always at work in human social and political experience.

The Deuteronomistic style cannot be pinned down to a single concept or metaphor, as the variety of commentary addressed above shows. Yet that there is a coherent worldview at work in the Deuteronomistic books is also clear from the way in which these commentators explore the nature of Deuteronomy as a totality and trace the echoes of its thought in the histories of Joshua to 2 Kings.

Israel's identity

At the heart of this continuity is the subject of Israel's identity, an identity presented in the Deuteronomistic books in certain key ideas which turn on the notion of unity and oneness. In Deuteronomy there is only one God in view, a focus which is supported by the law of the central sanctuary. There is only one lawful site for religious worship; keeping to that site will prevent Israelites from straying into the worship of other deities. As there is only one God so there is only one nation. All Israelites are neighbours and should support one another, a notion illustrated by the law of the tithe whereby other tribes give firstfruits to Levi in return for that tribe's priestly work on the behalf of All-Israel. The single deity at the heart of this picture is characterized by concern for the weak and the free gift to them of life and living. Israel is characterized as a nation chosen by God and gifted with a place of their own (McConville, 1993, p. 133). Israel's identity, therefore, stems from the role which God intends it to have. Israel is meant to be a witness to God's own character, by its faithfulness in mirroring divine intentions through its maintenance of a proper social system.

The Deuteronomistic Histories

All these patterns flow into the historical themes of Israel and its land, its leaders and its fate. Deuteronomy provides a set of concepts with which to measure and evaluate the meaning of historical events. Deuteronomy 28 lays out two ways before Israel in the land, the way of success (blessing) and the way of failure (cursing). The continual failure to worship YHWH properly, as depicted in the Deuteronomistic Histories, leads to Israel's failure to hold onto its land. 2 Kings' presentation of an ultimate separation between king and God after the rule of Manasseh prepares the reader for the invasion of Judah and for the deportation of its inhabitants.

In this manner Deuteronomy provides a backdrop of political theology in front of which events in time take place and in relation to which they can be measured. This is the basis of the link between Deuteronomy and the Deuteronomistic Histories: a constitution for Israel, set out, only partially achieved in time and place and finally annulled (McConville, 1993, p. 122).

Torah as social order

The tension between individual stories of people and events in Israelite history and a core collection of interpretative principles by which to evaluate these stories raises the wider issue of constitutional principles in the Deuteronomistic texts. The constitutional idea in these works is attached to the subject of Torah (Law) and Covenant. God makes a treaty with his people. The entire shape of Deuteronomy is similar to treaty format in the ancient Near East. There is a historical prologue rehearsing the benefits of the contract in the past before its current conditions are set forth in chapters 12–26, and the sanctions against covenant violation are established in chapters 28–29.

D. J. Elazar has examined this paradigm of a covenant political formula in relation to the political theology of biblical Israel. In *Covenant and Polity in Biblical Israel* (1995), he argues that

> The purpose of the Bible is to teach humans the right way to live in this world . . . The Bible discusses a whole range of subjects: the organisation of the Israelite polity, rules of war, ritual laws of public sacrifice, the method of providing for the poor and less fortunate . . .
> (Elazar, 1995, p. 62)

Elazar sees this as the basis for a proper understanding of a social order which exists because God loves Israel and wants it to be happy. The same loving loyalty should colour human responses to the covenant order and to God (Elazar, 1995, p. 71). The mutual support and dependency fostered by loyalty-based relationships prevents the destruction of peace and the slide into violent aggression. What is at issue is not simply personal freedom but a freedom sensitive to, and governed by, the interests of one's fellow citizens (Elazar, 1995, p. 71).

The theocratic state

Elazar argues that a covenantal constitution rests on three fundamental principles: theocracy, federalism and republicanism. Among these three subjects it is the theme of theocracy which is important for a consideration of the theology of the Deuteronomistic texts (Elazar, 1995, p. 354). The theocratic principle has the effect of putting politics into a fresh perspective in which it is no longer the preserve of human beings and their social choices. The state does not exist as an end in itself (Elazar, 1995, p. 354). By derivation political institutions do not serve the state but offer a means by which people allied with God can also be allied with each other. This entails the establishment of God's Holy Commonwealth or Kingdom on Earth as a primary goal of the Israelite nation.

Theocratic principles ensure that the state must be viewed as a moral entity. Its structures need also to be moral and to inculcate moral ideals and moral actions on the part of citizens. Different political forms serve this moral goal at different times in biblical Israel's life. But at each shift of government style the texts reiterate the basic concept of theocracy. Thus, when Joshua is about to die he calls the people together to Shechem (Jos 24) to renew the covenant with God and with one another. Likewise the institution of Saul as king is marked by a commentary which links this event to the overarching rule of God (1 Sam 11). Finally, the establishment of a Temple state in Judah in the Persian period is accompanied by a reading of the law of the divine covenant to which the people pledge obedience (Neh 8) (Elazar, 1995, p. 360).

Summary

Elazar's commentary on religion and politics in biblical Israel offers the reader a particular perspective on biblical ideology. It is the interpretation of someone who traces a clear line of continuity between ancient Israel and modern Judaism and who finds the inspiration for that Judaism in ancient religious tradition. Likewise, McConville and Millar, and Mason offer their chosen pathways into the Deuteronomistic texts, and each of their interpretations has its own ideological stance. Mason fits the Deuteronomistic books into the concepts of propaganda and subversion with which he critiques the entire OT collection. Propaganda for him means political propaganda, literature used to support particular political goals (Mason, 1997, p. 3). Subversion is defined in opposition to the term 'propaganda' and concerns the manner in which texts undermine those very political structures which they set out to uphold (Mason, 1997, p. 5).

McConville and Millar have a very different intention in their study. They are concerned with textual study and its relationship to theology. They focus on the method of redaction criticism, by which a text is viewed as an entity since that is the format which has come down to modern readers from the ancient editors. This scheme of thought allows them to view Deuteronomy as a whole and to highlight the balance in the text between the ideology of a fixed identity for people and land and that of the constant call to rely only on God and to sit lightly with regard to themes of centralized order such as that provided by the city, Jerusalem (McConville and Millar, 1994, p. 13).

What all these modern writers offer the reader is a variety of Deuteronomistic theologies, parallel means of gaining a sense of the message of the Deuteronomistic books. These theologies themselves project alternative ideological stances for readers' evaluation. Engaging with this material, readers give shape to their own basic response to the text and thus form personal ideologies. In this way the biblical texts provide a foundational picture of the constitutional identity of Israel, in the past, and also offer some constitutional principles which readers can adapt to new historical contexts.

10

The character of God

The previous chapter ended with the assertion that one possible manner of investigating the theological themes of the Deuteronomistic Histories is to consider in a detailed way God and Israel who are the partners in the biblical theme of covenant treaty which plays a significant part in these texts. This chapter will examine the nature and character of the God who is pictured in the Deuteronomistic works.

God is clearly a central figure in these texts overall, since it is he who has set the Deuteronomistic story in action by rescuing the Israelites from slavery in Egypt and who continues to shape the story by aiding the Israelites in their settlement in the Land. Within this overarching narrative, however, God is often not directly involved in the individual stories which make up whole books. God can and does speak to his people, usually through their leaders, but he is also a figure spoken about, someone whose character emerges from the voice of the narrator as much as from the narrative action.

God and the Deuteronomistic story

In Joshua, God appears to be the ultimate source of events but he operates largely through Joshua himself. The Lord spoke to Joshua who carried out his commands, is the way that the story presents events. Thus the conquest of Canaan is carried out by Israelite troops who are themselves the agents of an invisible deity. In Judges the close relationship of God with one leader is lost. God still speaks to Israel, but a gap opens up. Israel has lost a sense of God's immediate presence and does not carry through all that God wills. Yet God still listens when the Israelites cry to him in distress and answers their pleas by raising up temporary leaders. But direct speech between God and human beings seems to be broken apart since heavenly intermediaries are used to announce divine plans. As in the story of Samson's birth, an angel of the Lord appears to stand in for God. In Judges 13 Samson's father-to-be even doubts that the figure who appears really does come from God. The absence of God from the text comes to a climax in the last chapters of the book (chs 17–21), where many evil events occur as the characters pursue their own aims without reference to God.

God's direction of affairs emerges again in 1 and 2 Samuel. God raises up a prophet/judge in Samuel, calling him to his task while he is still a boy. God is physically present with Israel's army again in the Ark of the Lord which acts as the Israelite standard. Finally God chooses to lead Israel through a deputy – a king. Yet God does not speak directly to the king but addresses him through an intermediary, a court prophet such as Nathan who passes on to David the divine promise of a royal covenant and also tells him of God's judgement against him on account of his adultery with Bathsheba.

By contrast God does speak directly with Solomon, David's successor. He answers Solomon's prayers both at his succession and when he consecrates the Temple which he has had built for God. The death of Solomon paves the way for the ultimate separation of interest between God and people. Kings, both of Israel and of Judah, choose to worship other gods and although the Davidic line is preserved till the sixth century BCE, this is because God remembers his past intimacy with David rather than because of any close relationship between God and people in the present. In the last chapters of Kings it is the anger of God which stands out in the narrative. As for instance in 2 Kings 23:26–27, where 'the Lord did not turn from the fierceness of his great wrath . . .'.

In this material God performs different functions in the text, in relation to his people. He is their ultimate sovereign Lord and as such is the Judge of their acts. His role in the first four of the Deuteronomistic Histories is as a warrior leader whose symbolic presence in the Ark brings Israel victory. Charismatic power from God enables Israelite leaders to be powerful rescuers of the nation's fortunes, as in the exploits of Samson. God as royal councillor is a feature of the reigns of Saul and David, where prophets bring divine advice to the king's ears. God as prosecutor of a lawsuit against his people is what becomes of the prophetic voice in Kings, where Elijah, for instance, conducts a battle against royal religious policy.

The Lord of Israel

So far the term 'God' has been used, in this chapter, without elaboration as to the content of that term. But the question arises, which God does the text deal with? Any deity? A God with a particular name? The English word 'God' is used in the Revised Standard Version to translate the Hebrew term 'El'/'Elohim'. El is both the name of a particular deity, as found in the religious stories on clay tablets dug up by archaeologists in modern Ras Shamra (ancient Ugarit) in north-west Syria, and a generic term for a divine being. When translators put in the word 'God' then, they are rendering the second meaning of the Hebrew term. But this is not the only designation for God in the OT. Ultimately it is one particular deity whose nature is revealed by the texts – namely the God of Israel. In Exodus 3, Israel's God reveals himself by his own Name to Moses, by the name YHWH. This name is derived from the word 'to be' and indicates that God is connected with life/existence. Since Jewish law forbids the naming of God by a reader, for the Name is too holy to be pronounced in any normal circumstances, the Revised Standard Version, among other English versions, translates YHWH by the word 'LORD'. 'LORD' translates *Adonai*, a term regularly substituted for the real Name by a reader of the Hebrew Scriptures when encountering the Divine Name in the text.

The Lord of Israel is, then, the god whom the reader is really concerned with. Other gods are mentioned in the Deuteronomistic works usually as outsiders, gods of the nations and so alien to the Israelites. Israel's God is the God of the Fathers, of Abraham, Isaac and Jacob and the God of Moses. In the overall perspective of the OT it is this God, in Genesis 2, who is responsible for the creation of the earth and for the creation of human beings to cultivate it.

The Lord of the covenant

In the Deuteronomistic books God expresses this relationship with Israel in the form of a treaty whereby he promises to protect the people. God's character is revealed through these commandments, set out in Deuteronomy, as one of justice and concern for all his people, however weak or powerless. The covenantal aspect of God is given a further dimension in the Deuteronomistic Histories, when God promises David that he will be a father to David's son. God will establish an eternal covenant with the Davidic line of kings, provided that they remain faithful to God on their part. Whereas the Mosaic covenant reveals the Lord of Israel to be a god of law and commandment, the Davidic covenant shows God adopting kings into a family relationship with himself. Thus two aspects of God's character emerge – justice and friendship. This leads the reader to the further question, does God in the Deuteronomistic texts have a particular character and personal identity?

God and character

J. Miles, in his book *God: A Biography*, suggests that three aspects of God's character are developed by the Deuteronomistic texts. These three are conqueror, father and arbiter. They sit within the over-arching theme of God as master and ruler (Miles, 1995, p. 150). Miles argues that the character of God develops these functions as a response to the needs of his chosen people. God knows that he will need to protect Israel by the use of force, as he does in engaging in a contest with Pharaoh in order to free Israel from slavery. However the Canaanites, unlike the Egyptians, are not oppressors of Israel; they are killed rather to remove temptation from Israel's path. The extermination of Canaanites creates an image of God which is harsh and brutal. 'This mood of brutality gradually darkens and by the end of the book of Judges affects relations even among the twelve tribes of Israel' (Miles, 1995, p. 152).

The harshness is balanced by God's role as father to Israel. In Hannah's song (1 Sam 2) the themes of war and kindness are linked. God is appealed to as 'Lord of Hosts', that is, as warrior, but viewed as one who acts for the weak against the strong. The military component in his identity remains dominant, but a sub-theme of social concern begins to complicate that identity. According to Miles that tenderness blossoms, in 2 Samuel, into God's self identification as a father to Solomon. A father is always a father even if he rejects his son. So God commits himself to Solomon for good and for evil (Miles, 1995, p. 170).

God loves David and Solomon as a man loves his sons, but he is also committed to disciplining them and their heirs as a father corrects his sons. The fulfilment of fatherhood on God's part leads him to abandon his people and hand them over to hostile forces in the Assyrian and Babylonian conquests. But, whereas God as ruler could abandon Israel forever, God as father will reactivate his love and his promises and engineer the return of the exiles to their land. In order to achieve both discipline and renewal of relationship, God will act as arbiter, organizing the affairs of many nations, not only those of Israel, his people (Miles, 1995, p. 189).

In Miles' account, God is presented as a character who develops in relationship with a people. In the Deuteronomistic books he begins as a bellicose warrior whose personality shifts to one of intimacy and then to a measured control of universal destiny. The tempering element here is love. W. Moran (in Greenspahn (ed.) 1991) takes up the issue of God and love and compares the love of God with the covenant ideology of the ancient Near-Eastern texts which offer a background to Israelite thought. He points out that God's love is set against Israel's love. 'Love in Deuteronomy is a love that can be commanded. It is also a love intimately related to fear and reverence' (Moran, 1991, p. 104). In Egyptian treaties a similar love also binds sovereign and vassal (Moran, 1991, p. 105). For Moran, then, God's love in a Deuteronomistic setting is ultimately tied to the political framework of relationship between people and deity (Moran, 1991, p. 107). Moran's belief that the emphasis lies on loving loyalty and duty resulting from a formal contract between two parties is in line with Miles' comment that the Deuteronomistic god acts as a Liege Lord before any other function.

God the Divine Warrior

In Deuteronomistic thought the loving face of a covenantal deity has, paradoxically, the aspect of a god of warfare and bloodshed. T. Longman III and D. G. Reid have explored the presentation of God as a divine warrior. In *God Is a Warrior* (1995), they take as starting point the emergence of God as warrior in the scenes of Israel's escape from Egypt. Following that event, and especially in the settlement of the Land, Israel's God functions frequently as a warrior, an army leader (Longman and Reid, 1995, pp. 34–5). God as object of worship is equated with a god of warfare and in line with this identification the Ark of the Lord is carried into battle as a standard for Israel (Longman and Reid, 1995, p. 40). Since God has chosen the battle and marched out before his armies, God also claims all the spoils of battle for himself. Not only that, but in the law of the Ban (*herem*) all human beings captured in the war must be 'dedicated to God', that is, slaughtered in God's Name.

F. M. Cross has suggested in *Canaanite Myth and Hebrew Epic* (1973) that behind the historical face of Holy War lies the theme of creation-conquest, in which God creates by winning the battle against chaos. He notes that the Holy War theme is characterized by cosmic elements – on the one hand the title of Lord of Hosts refers to God's control of Israelite armies, on the other to God's heavenly forces. By defeating Israel's enemies, God restores order to creation and renews its stability just as he did in the original cosmic battle. In this case, however, the context is an historical land and the characters in the war are all human beings, Israelites and Canaanites. At this point Divine Warrior language becomes metaphorical. A stable society in its own land is symbolic of creation order and triumph over local enemies reflects divine triumph over the waters of chaos (cf. Gen 1:1–3).

Holy War language thus takes on a social function in society. By acting as a warrior, God presides over the establishment of a society and over its institutions. When the Lord of Israel assists Saul or David, the role of king is to be subordinate to that of the divine warleader, acting as his deputy. Holy War becomes, in this way, part of royal ideology, an image of God which supports royal power and links it to God's reign in the universe (Cross, 1973, p. 108). Treating God the warrior as a religious symbol used by society to express its values and beliefs may calm down the violently bloodthirsty picture of God created by the Deuteronomistic use of this motif which, because of its historical character, appears to endorse the brutal annihilation of enemies so long as this is justified by recourse to religious belief. But the problem of God and violence remains an issue for discussion.

God and violence

S. Niditch argues in *War in the Hebrew Bible* (1993), that the violence in the OT has inspired many acts of violence on the part of its readers across the centuries (Niditch, 1993, p. 4), thus it is necessary to come to grips with violence as an aspect of God's character. Niditch approaches the subject of the Ban from the perspective of sacrifice, first of all (Niditch, 1993, p. 50). A culture which thought of its God as requiring human sacrifice, including child sacrifice, could view the Ban sacrifice as another aspect of sacrificing to one's God, within the image of God as a being who requires blood sacrifice rituals. There is some evidence in the OT that parts of Israelite culture may have viewed God in this way. The evidence is mainly in terms of disagreement, such as Isaac's release from a sacrificial death in Genesis 22 and the Deuteronomistic condemnation of the child sacrifices of its time. But condemnation would not be necessary unless such acts were indeed carried out. In avoiding a sacrificial meaning to the Ban, the Deuteronomistic texts appear to reinterpret the Ban as a form of God's justice.

This is the context for Deuteronomy 13:12–18, where the Ban is used against fellow Israelites who commit abomination by worshipping other gods and being faithless to Yahweh. The emphasis here lies on God as a just deity who requires strict order and discipline from his people. Those who suffer bring the pain on themselves by inappropriate behaviour. However 'the ban as God's justice is a controversial and dangerous ideology, clothed in the respectable concept of covenant' (Niditch, 1993, p. 68).

Once the principle is agreed human beings can operate the system themselves with violent consequences. Thus, in Judges 19–21, justice seems to go awry. The story of the Levite's woman draws on the principle of necessary violence to restore order in society. The story itself is brutal, however, and the response of Israel likewise leads to more and more violence. Niditch states that ultimately it is God who presides over the slaughter and violence here, since all aspects of the text refer back to an image of the deity which involves divine acceptance of the role of warfare and bloodshed. It may even be that the use of the Ban for justice purposes has a more degrading influence than its use as sacrifice (Niditch, 1993, pp. 71–7). In this context God's role as Divine Warrior has ambiguous value. It is an image of strength and authority, but also invokes violence of a potentially unlimited scope since the God of Israel is himself a figure of unlimited power.

The development of God

Miles also comments on the bloodthirstiness of God in his war against Egypt and Canaan, but views this as a stage in the development of God's character in the OT as a whole. A further question emerges here, namely whether the God of Israel is a single figure, fixed from eternity.

On first reading of the OT, God is encountered as a single deity without a divine family, usually defined by male imagery, operating in a male authority role. Certainly that is the kind of God met with in the Deuteronomistic Histories. But is that the whole story or is there room for viewing the Lord of Israel as a deity conceived of in differing ways at separate stages in Israelite tradition? This matter is particularly relevant for a reading of the Deuteronomistic books, since emphasis is placed in these texts on the single God of

Israel versus the deities of Canaan who are regarded as false deities. Israel's sin is pictured as involving worship of these inauthentic gods.

But archaeological discoveries over recent years have shed some doubt on this picture as historically and culturally accurate. To imagine that the Deuteronomists represent an Israel of strict monotheism, a monotheism proclaimed by Moses and vital to Israelite identity from the beginning of nationhood, is subject to critique. R. Gnuse has surveyed the relevant evidence in his book *No Other Gods* (1997). He comments that 'Archaeologists are unearthing testimony of extensive Israelite devotion to Asherah, the goddess of fertility, and other gods of Canaan' (Gnuse, 1997, p. 69). Gnuse discusses the range of scholarship on this subject from those who argue that monotheism is a late post-exilic development, such as M. Smith, to those who uphold the view that Moses did indeed introduce monotheism to early Israel, such as J. De Moor. Gnuse concludes that the probability is that Israelite religion developed over time within the over-arching traditions of Syro-Palestinian religion (Gnuse, 1997, p. 124).

In this context there is an over-arching polytheistic tradition of religion in Syro-Palestine from the Bronze Age to the sixth century BCE, though each national group would have had its own particular patron gods and local rituals. Since the Deuteronomistic Histories refer to the separate states of Israel and Judah in the ninth to the sixth centuries BCE, each of these kingdoms would presumably have had its own local version of a Yahwistic religious system. As regional religion developed, first monolatry and then monotheism emerged within Israelite culture.

The aniconic tradition

One particular aspect of the development of the images of God in Israel is connected with the first command contained in the Decalogue and endorsed by the Deuteronomists, that there shall be no making of graven images of God. This command is called by scholars the aniconic tradition since there are to be no icons, no copies, of God's likeness. It has often been held that the Israelite aniconic tradition represents a hidden and transcendent God who is beyond all images, and a religious tradition which has passed beyond primitive superstition to a rational, philosophical religion.

B. Schmidt has recently pointed out that the biblical commands against imaging God are only part of the biblical picture (in

Edelman (ed.), 1995). In 2 Kings Josiah removes Nehushtan from the Temple. This appears to have been an object of worship and refers to the serpent image made by Moses as a means of healing Israelites in the wilderness. Josiah also removed the chariots and horses of the sun which Judahite kings had placed in the Temple. Both of these references imply the existence in the Jerusalem Temple of cult objects which allowed the worshipper to access the presence of YHWH. Schmidt argues that cultic references in the OT imply the existence of items which imaged God to the worshipper (Schmidt, 1993, p. 93).

Schmidt climaxes his description of ancient Israelite views of God with reference to the Kuntillet Arjud inscription. This is a drawing on an ostracon (potsherd or tile) of two gods, one larger and male, the other smaller and imaged with breasts. The inscription reads 'To YHWH and his Asherah' and the fragment belongs to the region of Israel in the monarchic period. This discovery raises the issue of God as a single being in the worship of ancient Israel. Here God apparently has a consort, Asherah being a well-known Palestinian fertility goddess. It seems that some ancient Israelites saw no problem in imaging YHWH as one deity among a pantheon of divine beings. The Deuteronomistic attack on these varied images of God then represents a religious reform of a later stage, with the YHWH-alone party arguing its case against the weight of older tradition.

God and sexuality

If God is regarded as a personal being, with an identity of his own, the question arises as to the role of sexuality and gender in relation to the deity. Human persons are to some extent defined by their sexual identity, so what about the Lord of Israel? In the Deuteronomistic books, God is a single male figure who is not sexually active. Thus there is an emphasis on the singleness of Israel's God. In a sense YHWH surpasses human physicality and is a timeless transcendent being. However, as has been shown above, the texts also image him in a very physical way, as a divine warrior, for instance. There is some ambiguity here which needs to be addressed.

W. Brueggemann discusses the theological issues raised by the matter of God and sexuality in his book, *A Social Reading of the Old Testament* (1994). He points out that twentieth-century American biblical scholars such as G. E. Wright have sought to argue that Israel's religion was imageless and speculative as opposed to the imaged and concrete presentation of God in Canaanite religion (Brueggemann, 1994, p. 150). However, Brueggemann notes that 'in a search for effective symbols we are inevitably drawn into the issue of *masculine/feminine* symbols . . . we are inevitably drawn into the issue of masculine/feminine imagery' (Brueggemann, 1994, p. 151).

Brueggemann seeks to bring together these two strands of asexuality and masculine/feminine imagery for God by picking out, from the work of scholars such as C. Westermann, the themes of salvation and blessing. He suggests that both ways of operating belong to the character of Israel's deity, but that blessing could be aligned with the feminine aspect of God and salvation with the masculine side. This method allows both sexual and asexual strands to have equal weight as descriptions of God. Brueggemann points out the need to include feminine models for God, since in past theological discussions, asexual imagery has so often turned into masculine imagery.

God and body

A further dimension of sexuality is that of body. Every sexual being has a bodily form within which and by means of which identity is expressed. The Deuteronomistic texts image God as a gendered being by their use of masculine pictures for God. Does God, then, have a body? The Deuteronomistic writers often seem to be unhappy with this idea. God's presence is expressed more through his Name than through an anthropomorphic presentation. H. Eilberg-Schwartz addresses this issue in his paper 'The problem of the body' (in T. K. Beal and D. M. Gunn (eds), 1997). He argues that Deuteronomy 4:12–24 suggests that God is bodiless – a voice heard from the midst of fire. Other OT texts, however, do speak anthropomorphically about God, texts such as Exodus 24:9. There is a tension here which highlights the ambiguity of the body itself.

If human beings are created in God's likeness but God does not have a body, then 'human embodiment and sexuality . . . are products of God's creative activity. Yet at the same time they are the very symbols of human difference from God' (Eilberg-Schwartz, 1997, p. 45). Eilberg-Schwartz reflects on the paradox of bodily existence for human beings and also for God. He remarks on the number of times in the OT that human beings see only the back of God and not his front. In 1 Kings 19 Elijah does not see God at all, since when he hears the still small voice he wraps his face in his mantle before going to encounter the divine presence. This motif of not seeing God face to face reflects the holiness and transcendence of the deity, but is there more to it than that? Could it be that this is a device to protect God's nakedness, just as Noah's nakedness, when he gets drunk on new wine, must be covered up by his sons (Gen 9:20ff.).

If God is anthropomorphically treated in this device, then God has a male body which needs to be covered from shame just as the human body does. This speculation allows an honourable place for human bodies, but raises questions about the use of sexuality.

> If God has no sex, then the reproductive organs of both males and females are rendered problematic. And if God does not have a sex, whether male or female, God's reproductive organs are useless. (Eilberg-Schwartz, 1997, p. 48)

These questions relating to divine sexuality arise out of the manner in which the OT speaks of God.

God is primarily a personal being, with a particular Name, and capable of being referred to by human male imagery, as in the warrior description. Covenantal theology itself implies God's personal existence, since it is hard to make a covenant with disembodied forces. A treaty format takes it for granted that the partners to the agreement know each other's characters sufficiently to be able to rely on the loyalty of the other. If God is imaged in a bodily manner, however, difficulties as well as advantages arise for the reader since such imagery is gender specific. But if God is disembodied is God capable of committing God's self to an alliance with a particular group of human beings?

God and history

The discussion of God's character in relation to body and sexuality cannot easily be resolved in favour of any one particular solution to the problematical issues. By contrast it may appear more useful to define YHWH through his connection with broad issues of time and space. Since the books from Joshua to 2 Kings present themselves to the reader as historiographical writing, the God whom they describe is, by derivation, a god of time and history. H. W. F. Saggs points out in 'The Divine in history' (in Greenspahn (ed.), 1991) that the concept of time used by the Deuteronomistic writers to structure their characterisation of the deity often appears to be cyclical.

There appears to be, in the texts, the working out of a divine plan. God plans Israel's conquest of the Land and continuously intervenes to promote that purpose even through the reigns of kings inimical to him. This could be presented as a key element of the theological presentation of God in the Deuteronomistic books. God uses history as his self-expression. Saggs points out that scholars such as W. Lambert have argued that the working out of the divine plan in history is an original theological insight in Israelite culture. However, late Assyrian texts contain similar ideas; Sargon II, for example, claimed that the god Ashur was using him as the means of achieving the divine purposes (Saggs, 1991, pp. 32–3).

The characterization of God in this way forms part of a wider ancient Near Eastern theological perspective. What is specific, for the Deuteronomistic writers, is the name of the deity concerned and the fact that this deity is involved solely with the plan for Israel and for no other people. Only at the far end of the Deuteronomistic theological perspective does YHWH take on the role of arbiter of the destinies of all the nations, but even then the spotlight is on what this entails for Israel and Judah in the way of rescuing them from humiliation and loss of identity.

The Deuteronomistic God

When readers of the books from Joshua to 2 Kings encounter God they meet the Lord of Israel. As was shown earlier in this chapter, the term 'God' here refers not to divinity in general but to one individual deity, with a name which has special meaning and who is pictured in the texts as the patron deity of one ancient society. The Deuteronomistic image of God is fashioned by the ancient writers who expressed their society's understanding of its God. The modern reader has to enter into dialogue with this God and to investigate his nature, seeking meaning from a knowledge of the ancient world. This is certainly true of the violent characteristics attached to Israel's God, for instance. Since social groups in different time periods have different worldviews, the task of adjusting to the ancient Israelite approach to God may offer a challenge to the modern reader.

11

The personhood of Israel

The previous chapter reflected in detail on the nature and identity of God in the Deuteronomistic Histories. It was clear, there, that the God referred to in these texts is the Lord of Israel. This means that God is inherently defined in relationship to human beings, in particular to the nation of Israel. It is appropriate, therefore, that a further theological matter to be explored is the nature and identity of the Israel which is the deity's covenant-partner in Deuteronomistic thought.

Biblical Israel

The term 'Israel' is used in the Deuteronomistic books to refer to a particular society made up of twelve tribes. But the root meaning of the term goes back before this to the story of Jacob in Genesis. As an older man, Jacob is told by God to return from exile to his own people and to meet again his brother Esau whose birthright-blessing he had stolen years before. On the journey back to his own people Jacob stops for the night at the river Jabbok, and here encounters God in the form of a mysterious stranger with whom he wrestles. As a result of this contest, God renames Jacob 'Israel' that is, he who strives with God. The name is renewed in Genesis 35:11-12, where God also promises 'a nation and a company of nations shall come from you'. From this beginning comes the term 'Israel' for a nation, since Jacob's twelve sons produce families who make up the later twelve tribes of All-Israel. Israel, then, is a name taken from a favoured ancestor, and membership of the group so defined is linked with genealogical descent from that ancestor. The tribes of Israel, as an extended family group with Jacob, go down to Egypt and there expand to become the 'hosts' of Israel who finally come up from Egypt to freedom. Israel is now a nation in the making, but not finally established until it has a land of its own. Thus Joshua marks the beginning of a new stage in Israel's identity as a nation.

Joshua to 2 Kings narrates the destiny of that chosen nation from start to finish. The book of Joshua shows God providing a land for his people which they struggle to keep in Judges and 1 Samuel. The rise of Saul and David as leaders brings about the beginnings of monarchy, so Israel turns into a kingdom, which is united in 2 Samuel and 1 Kings under its great kings, David and Solomon. But the death of Solomon creates a fissure. Now 'Israel' becomes in fact the name for the northern tribes who establish their own kingdom, while the southern tribes, faithful to the Davidic house, constitute a separate kingdom of Judah. With the Assyrian invasion in the eighth century BCE, Israel as a name for a particular state disappears forever. Judah takes up the traditions of Israel and its name as the people chosen by YHWH, until it succumbs to the Babylonians.

Strictly speaking, Israel ceases to exist in the eighth century BCE, but the title 'Israel' becomes a theological title, symbolizing the values and worship system of a Yahwistic cult. Thus Judah can think of itself as Israel both before the Babylonian exile and afterwards, when a Temple state was established in the Persian province of Yehud (Judah). Those who collected and edited the OT books regarded themselves as the rightful inheritors of Israelite traditions, and as the people to whom the God of Israel continued to make promises of unity and identity in return for fidelity in worship. This symbolic use of 'Israel' has lived on both in Christianity and in Judaism. The essence of 'Israel' as a theological term, then, is its connection with one particular deity – the Lord of Israel.

The people of the Lord: basic principles

Israel is, in a basic manner, defined by God's own existence. It is a nation founded to be a servant of God. Theologically, Israel mirrors divine values and characteristics. W. Brueggemann has explored one aspect of this idea in his book *Old Testament Theology* (1992). He picks out as a starting point the aniconic tradition about God (a topic addressed in the previous chapter of this present book). To this key concept of God Brueggemann attaches the Ten Commandments, thus making a link between an image of God and an aspect of Israelite tradition. The counterpart of an aniconic deity is that 'Israel models, constructs, and advocates an ordering of human community that ... refuses to assign any visible structure, form or symbolisation to the power ... of holiness' (Brueggemann, 1992, p. 124).

The Lord of Israel appeared to Moses in a burning bush and, as a heavenly voice associated with fire, promised freedom for Israel to live in an alternative society to that of the Egyptian empire. Freedom and equality thus becomes principles which Israel should develop and cherish. The laws of the covenant help Israel to shape itself as a society which emerges from the basic premises of social equality. Thus law is viewed, by Brueggemann, as implementing a social policy which is part of Israel's destiny as a people. It is by keeping the covenant code, expressed in Exodus 21–23 and in Deuteronomy, that Israel will constitute itself as a people. When Israel chooses to keep the tenets of Law the people become most fully themselves, in freedom and equality, and fulfil the destiny which God has prepared for them. But Israel is continually tempted to express itself through fixed structures which can become oppressive. These structures may involve religion, as with the golden calf made by Jeroboam in 1 Kings 12, or they may be secular, as when kingship becomes the total expression of Israelite society.

Images and symbols have an ambivalent function. In 1 Kings 8 the Temple, in Solomon's prayer, is a fixed point for accessing Israel's God, but God has already pointed out to David, in 2 Samuel 7, the limitations of such a fixed symbol. God lives in the heavens and moves freely across time and space. God has migrated with Israel and does not need a fixed house to dwell in. Israel constantly has to learn the point that it is a nation created by a transcendent deity and, to some extent mirrors the divine transcendence by being called in each stage of its existence to view itself as distinct from its contemporary institutions and to be prepared to change structures in order to realign itself with its foundational principles. Thus Josiah, in 2 Kings 22, hearing the old law book read, realizes that there is a need for reform, for a renewal of Israel's identity, both secular and religious (Brueggemann, 1992, p. 133).

Insofar as all readers of the Deuteronomic books may associate with an Israel faithful to God, they too are called to own this identity and to make it visible in social and political issues of their own time. This is a socio-theological argument in which religious belief cannot be separated from everyday human activity. Brueggemann applies this reading of Israelite identity to the twentieth-century world in which readers of the OT are called, like Israel, to evaluate the social and political structures of their time (Brueggemann, 1992, p. 140).

Sacred traditions

In his exposition of this theological argument of the image-free nature of God and Israel, Brueggemann refers to ancient Israel as the people of Exodus-Sinai. By implication, here, Exodus-Sinai are tools for defining Israel. But what are these theological tools? They are the sacred traditions of ancient Israel which M. Noth thought were created long ago, at the time of Moses and Joshua, but which more recent scholarship considers to be the creation of a post-exilic Judah. Whichever approach is taken to that issue, the method of focusing upon sacred tradition as a source of identity is still valid. Noth argues (Noth, 1960, ch. 3) that these traditions included various scenes

- the deliverance from Egypt
- the patriarchs
- the Covenant of Sinai

and situates their social function at moments of covenant renewal such as is found in Joshua 24.

Joshua 24 contains references, given as part of a speech by Joshua, to these sacred traditions. In verses 2–4 Joshua speaks of the patriarchs, of Abraham, Isaac and Jacob. The God of Israel took these men away from worship of other gods and made them the ancestors of his own people. Verses 6–8 describe the Exodus from Egypt, verses 9–18 describe the campaigns by which Israel gained its land. Finally the chapter echoes the original contract-making between God and Israel at Sinai in the renewal of covenant through Joshua's mediation, set out in verses 19–28. In this section there are clear echoes of the language of Deuteronomy, whereby God is imaged as holy and jealous (verse 19). This chapter of Joshua, then, rehearses the themes which make up the sacred traditions of Israel, by which the nation identifies itself as linked to an image of a God who accompanies the people in their progress through history.

Israel as a nation

The picture presented in Joshua 24 is that of a nation aware of itself as an individual people, and aware of how it has been shaped by past events which led to the present reality. National awareness is both a positive and a negative concept. Positively it fosters unity and neighbourliness among those who view themselves as part of a common society, but it can also lead to xenophobia. Both tendencies are visible in the Deuteronomistic portrait of Israel.

In 'The problem with pagans' (in Beal and Gunn (eds) 1997) L. D. Hawk points out both aspects at work within the Deuteronomistic texts (Hawk, 1997, p. 153). On the one hand, Israel conquers Canaan with a violent invasion, on the other, outsiders are sometimes spared, as with Rahab and the Gibeonites, while insiders such as Achan are destroyed. Hawk enquires into the purpose of this style of writing, and concludes that the focus is not so much on annihilation of nations for its own sake, but rather on the insecurity of Israelite identity. Israel is to destroy that which is alien to it, in order that its own identity may be secured. Likewise, insiders who detract from the common laws which identify Israel must be wiped out. The nation must preserve its shape, its 'body' (Hawk, 1997, p. 155). Rahab and the Gibeonites are only preserved because they identify themselves as part of Israel. Rahab asks for a place in Israel once her city is taken and the Gibeonites are brought into Israel as servants of the people (Hawk, 1997, p. 156). Achan, on the other hand, becomes part of Canaan; the rocks piled on his grave becoming part of the landscape (Hawk, 1997, p. 160).

The Deuteronomistic theme of 'Israel alone' serves to create a clear sense of social solidarity and marks the boundaries of Israel's shape. Israel and Canaan function as theological symbols with which to measure national identity – those on the inside/those on the outside. However, actual membership of these units is blurred at the edges. Some of those who are outside can come in and some who are inside will be driven out. The narrative of events is in tension with the starkness of the foundational message. Us versus Them can sometimes, in everyday terms, mean Us and Them.

L. Rowlett picks up the same theme in an article on 'Inclusion, exclusion and marginality in the book of Joshua' (in Exum (ed.), 1997). Joshua appears, at first sight, to be a text which relates a simple national epic, the taking of Canaan, but it is in fact more subtle than this in its message, 'the focus throughout most of the book of Joshua is on the marginal cases, exploring the questions: who is included, who is excluded' (Rowlett, 1997, p. 63). For Rowlett the purpose of such a text is to have a particular effect on its readers. Interest is on 'the way that the text of Joshua . . . functions as an instrument of coercion . . .' (Rowlett, 1997, p. 63), through which the reader is encouraged to submit to the picture of Israelite identity portrayed in the text. The social function of the literature, here, is to support the view that Israel has a clear identity and so by derivation, the society of the writers and readers of the text should maintain a tight unity (Rowlett, 1997, p. 71).

Violence and revelation

W. Brueggemann also addresses the issue of the social violence pictured in the book of Joshua, especially in chapter 11. What could be the theological purpose of all that bloodshed? he asks. How can such material be treated as part of divine revelation? Brueggemann suggests that the most helpful method here is to consider the broad context of the chapter. Israel has been at the mercy of an empire and its resources. It has barely escaped oppression, and now faces other established states which once more threaten its survival. It is not surprising in such a social context that Israel looks forward, in a dream for the future, to the removal of alien cultures which threaten its freedom to exist (Brueggemann, 1994, p. 296). Revelation, understood as theological message, emerges here out of the heart of a social group's dreams and hopes for the future, rather than breaking in from the outside. The society's pictures of its own social identity form the basis of a theological statement about God. For God is the deity who can bring about the fulfilment of these ambitions (Brueggemann, 1994, p. 297). It is in this event of gaining space to exist that Israel comes to identify itself *vis-à-vis* God.

There remains some harshness here for all those who are judged to be enemies of liberation. God is in fact a God of force and authority. Violence cannot be totally removed from the text. Israel truly is a society formed from violent revolt against armed oppression whose security is achieved by further use of force. Where there is an oppressive system in existence, Brueggemann suggests, there exists also the possibility of its violent overthrow.

From nation to kingdom

Harshness is visible also in the last chapters of the book of Judges, where Israelites commit more and more violent acts against each other. These chapters serve, in the overarching shape of the Deuteronomistic narrative, as a bridge between charismatic leaders (judges) and established authority (kings). It has been suggested that they in fact serve as a prologue for kingship as the national institution of Israel. Where there is no king everyone is a law to themselves and so anarchy breaks out and social cohesion is lost. By contrast, kingship is a valuable institution which maintains group identity through its insistence on law and order.

W. J. Dumbrell, however, argues that this view is not certain (in Exum (ed.), 1997). In 1 Samuel, which follows Judges, doubt is cast on the value of kingship. It too can work against a clear sense of national identity and harmony within the group, by its oppressive and selfish tendencies. So what then could the message of these chapters be, concerning Israel's identity?

Dumbrell suggests that the text should be set in an exilic context. The exilic period was one in which there was no king, no Temple. In this setting, chapters 19–21 of Judges serve as a model of reassurance. In the past, in the transition from nationhood to kingdom, there had been a period of uncertainty when social chaos proliferated. But in the Deuteronomistic narrative as a whole the message is that this social anarchy did not last forever. As God was able to take the messiness and violence and turn it around in the past so, in a different age, God would again intervene to re-establish 'Israel' in a stable form. There is even the possibility that this text is pointing especially to the validity of a theocratic state (Dumbrell, 1997, p. 82).

Israel as a kingdom

What had, by the exilic period, been broken apart as the social identity of Israel – kingship – was only in embryo in Judges. Abinelech's attempt at royal rule ended in disaster, but the idea of kings as valuable aids to national identity was about to emerge fully, in 1 Samuel. There the Israelites demand to have a king like other nations. They see their nationhood as reaching its climax and fulfilment in the institution of monarchy.

Monarchy as a theological concept of Israelite identity is a mixed reality. Under David, monarchy is, indeed, the theological and social climax of Israel's growth to self-realization. But, on the other hand, 1 Samuel predicts a king exactly like all the other nations, that is, one who is oppressive of his subjects, and Solomon appears somewhat in that guise since he imposes such taxation and services on the tribes of the northern region of Israel that they decide to break decisively with the Davidic line, on his death. Both the advantages and the disadvantages of kingship are visible in the narratives about particular kings, though the ultimate message is that kings let Israel down. Deuteronomy acknowledges that kings will be part of Israel's system, but makes them into wise philosophers totally subordinate to the Torah laws. The Histories flesh out the story of actual kingship, which is not carried out according to the model in Deuteronomy (except for Josiah) and which carries both heights and depths of royal political styles.

It has been argued, by W. Brueggemann for instance, that the Deuteronomistic texts carry the traces of two cultural perspectives in relation to Israel and monarchy. The Davidic covenant material represents the royal ideology of Israel in which 'Israel' is a body constituted around palace and Temple. But a second and opposing tendency in the Deuteronomistic works is to critique that ideology via the model of Exodus / Sinai in which God is Israel's ruler and human leadership is not dynastic. The focus for Israel is the mobile Ark which travels with the people and symbolizes divine assistance, and the goal is a land where All-Israel can be free within the framework of laws emanating from YHWH's treaty with his chosen people.

Kings of Israel

Despite the limitations associated with kingship, however, this form of social organization does carry Israel's identity in some sections of the Deuteronomistic story, notably during the reign of King David. It is therefore reasonable to examine the manner in which kingship and national identity are linked in these texts. M. K. George introduces his paper on Davidic kingship, 'Assuming the body of the heir apparent' (in Beal and Gunn (eds), 1996), with the mixed perceptions of the role of kingship in Israel to the forefront. He argues that the OT produces a series of reflections on the meaning of 'Israel' and is entirely taken up in the enterprise of naming Israel (George, 1996, pp. 164–5). In this context the king is the mirror image of society; his body, his character, is intimately linked with that of Israel at large. The king is also an image of God for Israel, in that he stands in God's place as ruler of the people.

Insofar as Saul had such a role in Israel, it would be important for maintenance of his role that he handed on his task to his own son, the heir to his body. But the story told in the Deuteronomistic Histories involves a change of dynasty. David inherits the throne of Israel, not Jonathan. George points out how the text accommodates this shift while preserving the theological perspective on kingship as creative of Israel's identity. Jonathan and David are portrayed as intimate friends and so as 'brothers'. Both are, also, originally, closely linked to Saul, one as blood son, the other as 'adoptive son'. David's identity is thus interwoven with that of Saul's house. When, in 1 Samuel 18:4, Jonathan puts his cloak, armour, sword, bow and belt on David, he is emphasizing the oneness of David with himself. When Saul and Jonathan are killed in battle, David's lament over them (2 Sam 1:17–27) represents the lament for his household which a loyal son and brother would make. David, by these means, is inserted into Israelite history as the true heir to Saul. Thus kingship as an ideal for Israelite identity survives the discontinuity of changing households.

Together with David himself, Solomon is the other king in Israel who is presented in the Deuteronomistic books in a manner which indicates his function as a model for Israel. Solomon is the actual heir to David, though not without competition for the throne among his half-brothers. Solomon it is, though, who inherits the kingdom and establishes Israel as a powerful nation. In his reign the united kingdom of Israel reaches its greatest extent and power. At the heart of this model of Israel is the close relationship between God and king – a topic focused through the lens of wisdom. When Solomon 'became' Israel the first thing he asked for, in 1 Kings 3, was wisdom to govern his country.

W. Bruggemann comments on this imaging of Solomonic kingship from a socio-religious setting. What the image of Solomon accommodates is a shift in practical terms in Israelite society. Monarchical rule involves the establishment of centralized state government and it is in this way that the Deuteronomistic Histories treat Solomon's reign, as a time of centralizing of government on palace and Temple at Jerusalem (Brueggemann, 1994, p. 249). These changes have to be accompanied by intellectual shifts that create a context in the overall perceptions of reality suitable to carry and support technological and administrative change. In royal Israel these intellectual shifts are imaged in the immense wisdom of the ruler. Thus Solomon partakes in divine wisdom, as is made plain in the later tradition of the Wisdom of Solomon, where divine wisdom is asked for as a bride from heaven.

Prophets in Israel

The Deuteronomistic texts provide a critique to the royal model of Israelite identity through the role of the prophetic figures who serve as guides and as critics of how the king of Israel is living out his responsibilities. In his book, *Covenant and Polity in Biblical Israel* (1995), D. J. Elazar discusses these dual roles of king and prophet in Israelite monarchy. On page 308 he sets out a diagram showing the Deuteronomistic theory of kingly society, in which he argues that the Congregation of Israel is now built up from a system of balancing powers which work together in the united kingdom of David and Solomon. The main characters here are God, the king, the prophet, the high priest and the nation. This model can be viewed as secular, dealing with daily issues of government through the royal household, but also as theological, focused on the eternal deity from whom nationhood has come. Thus the people carry two roles – that of People of the Land and that of the Congregation of Israel, worshippers of YHWH.

In this context the role of a prophet such as Nathan, at David's court, is to hold the balance between the secular and religious aspects of Israel's identity. He offers a critique from God on David's plan to build a temple, in 2 Samuel 7, but in that same scene he also conveys the oracle of blessing on David's dynasty. With the career of Elijah in 1 Kings there is a difference. Elijah is in open opposition to the kings of Israel while they are turned away from a Yahwistic cult to the Baals of Israel's Syro-Phoenician neighbours. In this context the prophets are presented as bearing the identity of Israel, in opposition to royal figures who have lost the true meaning of kingship for Israel and have come to see power as their personal prerogative, to do with as they wish.

The prophetic contribution to Israel's identity is made clear in the story of Elijah's struggle with the prophets of Baal. J. T. Walsh, in his commentary on 1 Kings notes how one strand of the narrative involves the conversion of the people. 'At the beginning . . . several things identify the people with the Baalist position. Like Baal's prophets they limp, and like Baal himself they do not answer (vss 21 & 26)' (Walsh, 1996, p. 255). As the story progresses the people's attitudes change. They are prepared to accept Elijah's challenge, which opens them to the possibility of accepting YHWH as their God. Once Baal's prophets have failed they are called in the text to 'come near' and they do, thus symbolically moving towards a change of religious allegiance. 'Yahweh's spectacular acceptance of the offering brings the people to the choice they initially refused to make' (Walsh, 1996, p. 256). This short story indicates the way in which texts can carry theological purposes. In this case the narrative tells the reader once again that Israel's identity is sewn up with its deity.

The story of Ahab's seizure of Naboth's vineyard in 1 Kings 21 offers the other half of this picture of Israel's true character. Here Ahab symbolizes all that is wrong with kingship as a socio-political

expression of Israel. Personal gains have come to outweigh principles of justice. This way of being Israel is condemned by God
through the voice of the prophet. The reader is led via the act of
reading to a renewal of understanding about the manner of being
Israel (Walsh, 1996, p. 34).

Sin, repentance and identity

Once again the bottom line of meaning attached to the Deutero-
omistic texts is the theme of identity through social justice. W.
Brueggemann argued in 'Social criticism and social vision in the
Deuteronomistic formula' (in Brueggemann, 1994) ·that this is
linked with the motif of deed-consequence as a descriptor of events
in the life of Israel. This is made up of two parts (a) 'And Israel
sinned'/'did what was evil' . . . and (b) 'And the Lord' . . . (helped
Israel's enemies), and occurs regularly in the Deuteronomistic
style of theological writing.

This motif is balanced by another pair of terms: (c) 'Cry out'
and (d) 'Deliver'. Israel is imaged as a person who sins and then
cries out in anguish at the result of sin, just as God is a person
who punishes but also delivers. There is in these formulaic descriptions of Israel's identity an inherent tension. Israel cannot keep a
clear vision of its true self before its face and cannot recognize
what the practical expression of its ideals should look like in a
given situation. This theological message is often a suitable one
for actual experience. Life experience includes bad fortune and the
ideas of sin and repentance provide a reason for bad luck and a
means of dealing with it (Brueggemann, 1994, p. 89).

Fostering civic virtue

D. J. Elazar addresses the issue of how morality relates to civic
virtue – how broad principles take on specific meanings. He begins
from the context of the Deuteronomistic texts within the Hebrew
Bible, which incorporates them to prophecy as the Former Prophets and states that 'the central concern that binds all the historical
books together is the prophetic concern with the maintenance of
God's covenant with Israel' (Elazar, 1995, p. 281). In Joshua and
Judges the concern about covenant maintenance is expressed
through a republican form of government with leaders chosen for
their relationship with God but responsible to the people and the
Law. In 1 and 2 Samuel and 1 and 2 Kings it is a monarchical

government which must make concrete the same basic social values.

Israel as a moral person

The essence of Israel, therefore, is that it has a moral character. This essential morality must be expressed in political regimes as well as in individual lives. The working out of these moral themes is often done through stories, that is, through case studies, but there is nevertheless an underlying coherence across all the varied stories and examples. A critical reading of the Deuteronomistic books 'reveals what can be understood to be a number of serious discussions of the great questions of political morality' (Elazar, 1995, p. 237).

The bottom line of all the stories of men and women of Israel and of the nations, found in the Deuteronomistic Histories, is to point by different means to the overarching issue of Israel as a person – that is, as someone capable of acting responsibly and of having social rights and duties. Here the nation is viewed as a whole, as though it were a single being. And the essence of the personhood of Israel is its creation as a moral being, whose religious beliefs cannot be separated from its daily life and its relations with other nations on the international scene.

12

Conclusion

This book began by introducing the reader to the basic elements of the Deuteronomistic material. It explored, in the Introduction, the geographical and historical realities concerned with ancient Israel, and embarked on the task of a careful investigation of the Deuteronomistic books as works of literature. In coming to a conclusion it should be noted that some of the major issues relating to the Deuteronomistic texts have already been summarized. Thus, at the end of chapter 5, the relevance of biblical archaeology and the nature of history as a discipline of study were addressed directly.

It seems appropriate to balance the format of the Introduction which focused on the texts and their historical setting with a Conclusion which looks to the readers of the Deuteronomistic texts, more especially to modern readers. Texts are useless items when separated from their audience. As a means of communication between human beings literary works only come alive when the reader 'receives' them and appropriates a personal meaning from them. More recent critical methodologies highlight the significance of readers and their response as contributing to the meaning of the text itself. The historical-critical method turns rather to the ancient readers than to modern ones but it, too, looks for meaning in terms of a book's relevance for its audience. In connection with the Deuteronomistic texts the reader, ancient or modern, is responding to an historical text. But what does that mean for a reader; what perspective to reading emerges from defining a certain work as 'historical'?

Starting to read

The first step in a systematic exploration of the Deuteronomistic Histories is for readers to become acquainted with the narratives which make up these works. However, getting to know the story, on a surface level of reading, is simply a starting point for an exploration of meaning. The Deuteronomistic books are found, in the Hebrew Bible, in the position of bridge between Torah and the written books of prophecy. This shows that the compilers of the Hebrew Bible regarded the books from Joshua to 2 Kings as providing some of the groundwork for Israel's identity as a people in relationship to their God. But what exact groundwork was envisioned here? A modern reader might easily say, looking at the surface of the texts, the history of Israel. But this again raises the question, In what sense are the books historical works? A first stage in reading, then, leads on to a deeper engagement with the historical dimensions of the Deuteronomistic works.

Modern biblical criticism and a system of reading

Exploring the historical dimensions of the Deuteronomistic books is thus the first methodology modern readers encounter in their search for ways of examining the texts in detail. Modern biblical criticism has focused heavily on this approach, so what exactly is modern biblical criticism? The focus here is on finding the truth about the literature, which involves getting back to the original setting of the books and identifying the oldest material to be found in them. Scholars have argued that the texts of the OT have undergone a process of development over time, within ancient Israel, and that it is possible to trace, within existing texts, some of the original material which had been used by editors. This argument links with the view that there was a gradual process by which Israelite religion moved from oral to written forms. A method of study is proposed in which the reader aims to uncover the different layers of material in a text from the earliest sections through later additions to the final editing.

It could be argued, for instance, that a story such as that of Samson in Judges existed first as a separate cycle of folktales about a past hero, told by village storytellers. It would then move into written form and finally be incorporated into a longer text where it would be situated in a historical sequence. The entire Deuteronomistic books fall apart, following this method of interpretation, into separate incidents and scenes, often only a few verses in length. These represent what a storyteller might deliver on one occasion in a village gathering. This would be the core of the tale only, since each storyteller was free to flesh out the key elements of the tale with dramatic additions as the tale was narrated. These additions were usually omitted from the written account. Stories of battles and of past heroes and heroines fit in here.

At the same time, the references in the books of Kings to chronicles of events in the life of rulers implies the existence of earlier documentary sources which the writer is drawing on for his own account of the past. So from traditional units of material and from earlier written texts the editors produced the final version of the books as modern readers now encounter them. The work of the editor was to select which parts of traditional material to use and how to join them up with geographical and chronological phrases which set the scene for the next unit. As well as this the editor could add in his own theological interpretations of tradition. The recurring use of 'sin', 'cry out', 'deliver' phrases in Judges is an example of how an editor could structure text, holding togther disparate stories and giving them added meaning. On the one hand each deliverer has their own narrative, but, on the other, all are linked as examples of the deliverance theme.

This system of reading encourages the reader to search out earlier forms of the biblical text. However, since none of the earlier, shorter forms of such texts survive, usually, scholars can only speculate as to the exact nature of the development of literary traditions. As regards the Deuteronomistic Histories, the Introduction pointed to the foundational role of M. Noth in proposing a scheme for the development of the Deuteronomistic texts; it also pointed to the current critique of that proposal by G. Auld.

Further reading systems

But reading these texts as the result of an historical process of composition is only one method open to modern readers. Since the mid-1900s a good deal of unease with this method of reading the text has surfaced. In this book attention has been drawn to *The Post Modern Bible* – a study which investigates a wide range of alternative methodologies for reading the Old Testament.

A method of reading such as narrative criticism which focuses upon individual passages and their particular style often appears to be at odds with the search for the theological message of texts where theology is viewed as encompassing the whole of texts in a single level of meaning. For theological readings have tended to be wide-ranging and to have the effect of harmonizing variations in message across passages in order to make them fit into one paradigm, such as the treaty form of Covenant. A way forward here, which this book has utilized, was the method of ideological criticism. In this approach theology is identified with theory. Books convey ideas to their readers, ideas which, once owned by the readers, can be taken up by them in their own right.

All these methodologies are attempts to read and understand a given reality. What the reader is offered is a toolkit containing a number of different tools (methodologies), each of which can be used on the text with varying results in terms of the message which can be found within a given literary work. Once readers get started, then, there is not one single act of reading to be done but a number of separate readings can take place in relation to a single book.

All these reading activities are linked together because, in the end, they are connected to the same text. The text is the bottom line of reading. For modern readers a given text is met with as a sub-unit of a larger collection of books, labelled 'The Bible'. But this is not how the books emerged originally. They were not consciously written to accompany one another; the collecting came later. The ultimate level of reading, then, involves treating the texts as individual works. It entails an ability to read the material in its original language, in the case of the Deuteronomistic works in Hebrew. It also requires the reader to go back behind a modern version of a book to the individual manuscripts which are the evidence for the manner in which the text tradition of that book developed.

History and the reader

When a reader encounters a text which positions events in a sequence and tells the story of what happened in the past, it is easy for that reader to apply, even unconsciously, knowledge of what 'history' means in the twentieth century to an interpretation of the text. But this is a misleading exercise if it leads the reader to focus on an ancient book as though it were a modern documentary account of the past. Then, as now, ancient authors believed that the past was relevant for the present; they even had a greater appreciation of the value of tradition than many modern people do. The major Greek and Roman historians of the ancient world also believed in the value of checking sources and aiming for an accurate picture of events. But absolute accuracy of details within an account of the past was not as vital as that the relevance of the events in their longterm setting should be brought out by the historian's narrative.

Thus, a modern reader encountering the Deuteronomistic texts is correct in looking closely at the historical narrative format, because this is the format chosen by the Deuteronomistic writers to express their concept of God and society. However, this is not the same mode as documentary history. The intention here is to reveal divine activity and so flesh out the divine nature, rather than tell the human story for its own sake. It is perfectly possible that behind the existing stories of ancient Israel there are details stemming from a memory of an historical people in ancient Syro-Palestine, but that is not the main focus of the texts.

The first part of the present book explored some of the issues concerning the application of the modern term 'historically accurate' to Joshua to 2 Kings. For all these reasons caution must be exercised in treating the Deuteronomistic Histories as *the* history of Israel. However, the literature of the OT does use an historical approach to God. When the reader comes to use literary-critical and ideological-critical methods it is necessary to take seriously the literary presentation of God and Israel within a chronological framework. The texts create their own inner world, using geography and history to do so. History thus becomes a relevant concept for biblical Israel, the society portrayed within the texts. Using narrative and ideological methodologies a reader can justifiably say 'David said' or 'Solomon did', in the sense of talking about the David or Solomon of the texts. Whether actual kings of Israel did and said such things is a further issue, irrelevant for these methodologies, although it is at the heart of the historical-critical style of interpretation.

History and the Christian reader

For some readers the crunch comes over this matter of history and its connection with belief. If modern readers believe that the Deuteronomistic works express authentic ideas about the divine world and they associate that with modern scientific investigations of the past, then faith may come to depend on the view that every detail of the narratives actually happened at a set time in the past. To discover that the historical assumptions here cannot be scientifically proved to be true appears to threaten the sacred value of texts. But this problem is a modern one and turns on the variant meanings of the term 'history' in the ancient world and nowadays. What mattered in the ancient world was the underlying truth told by the story. In the Exodus event what matters is that God intervenes in the lives of human beings and can even free oppressed people from foreign domination. As a result of this evidence readers can understand why Israel is called to make a Treaty with YHWH and can, in each generation, renew a commitment to a covenant-God.

To put the matter crudely, whether the water on each side of the Israelites as they crossed over from Egypt was indeed a wall of water is of little importance in its own right. To tell the story of a wall of water is meaningful because it emphasizes the greatness of the threat and therefore the power of the Lord of Israel. It is also meaningful because water, in the OT, is often symbolic of chaotic forces, as in the beginning of Genesis 1. The writers believed that YHWH could and did control chaos and often referred symbolically to divine order as a putting down of mighty waters.

This manner of reading the text, looking for the symbols and reinterpreting the images, was the common method of interpreting the OT among the Christian writers and teachers of the early Christian centuries. Thus the story of the meeting of Abraham and God at Mamre in Genesis 18, was seen to contain hidden evidence of the trinitarian nature of God. This is possible as an explanation because the text jumps between God speaking as a single figure and the three strangers who approached Abraham. From the Christian perspective this meaning had always been in the text, but was never discovered until the right interpreters came along. The Christians were the inheritors of the OT and so were vouchsafed the true interpretation of the text by God. The text itself is open to other interpretations and clearly, Jewish rabbis have not given this meaning to the text, in their tradition. However, some Jewish writers of the first century CE did make use of a symbolic method of reading text. Thus Philo of Alexandria taught that the patriarchs up to Moses should be read not as historical characters but as symbols of everyman. Each patriarch represented a stage in human spiritual development, with Moses reaching the ultimate goal of companionship with divinity.

In all these methods an historical–literal approach was avoided. Indeed, in his *Confessions* Augustine of Hippo makes it plain that treating the historical aspects of texts such as the Deuteronomistic Histories as the main source of information about God was the greatest biblical obstacle to his own conversion. Only when some Christian Neo-Platonists taught him to read the Scriptures symbolically could he own the truth of biblical theology as a foundation for faith. Marcion, in the second century CE, even went so far as to label the God of the OT a demi-god and not the true creator of the world. This was an opinion he drew from, for instance, his literal reading of the Deuteronomistic God as a 'human' and flawed being caught up in historical events. Marcion's view was rejected by the mainstream Christian tradition, but it shows how little value early Christians placed on the historical level of text as the main strand for conveying theological truth.

Looking at these aspects of the tradition of Christian interpretation of biblical material makes the reader realize that reading is not a fixed and unchanging activity. Different generations of readers produce different methods of reading. Twentieth-century readers often begin their reading, in the contemporary world, from the perspective of modern biblical criticism and then branch out to further modern methodologies. Going back to the history of interpretation offers the reader a further dimension for exploring the meaning of texts.

The reader and the texts

The process of reading the Deuteronomistic books combines both simplicity and complexity. Ultimately, meaning in a textual context reduces to the 'words on the page', but, to own that meaning involves the reader in lines of thought which are complex and subtle. Ideas *about* the text cannot stand except insofar as they are confirmed by and from the words *of* the text. But the words of the text only gain depth and colour when they are explored in a broader context. Basic terms found in the Deuteronomistic books, such as 'God' and 'Israel' are simple delineators of characters in the story and yet they are also complex concepts in which several different meanings co-exist. 'God' as a character in the text is the particular Lord of Israel and yet is also the God of all the readers who read the Deuteronomistic narratives with some belief in the relevance of this material to their own lives. 'Israel' indicates an ancient nation, but all readers can choose to align themselves with the Israel of the story – or not. Israel and its deity can be pinned down in time to the conceptual framework of writers of the sixth century BCE or can be set alongside archaeological evidence of habitation in ancient Syro-Palestine. They can also be opened up to consist of the timeless God of the 'Israel' of every age in which the texts are still read and accepted as meaningful for readers.

The text is a static, fixed reality, just words, until the imagination of the reader renders it alive and makes it a dynamic force in shaping the future by allowing a reading of its narrative to influence contemporary understanding of life experience. It is this convergence of text and meaning via the reader that is the starting point for the present study. Biblical Israel (Deuteronomistic texts) both reflects and paves the way for historical Israel (the historical writers of those texts/their historical readers). Historical Israel gave birth to biblical Israel in the creation of the Deuteronomistic Histories, and provides biblical Israel with a future existence through the handing down of biblical tradition across the human generations of readers each in their own time period. Biblical Israel is kept alive by the preservation of the relevant literature and, in turn, it gives rise to a new form of 'historical Israel' as a fresh group of readers interpret their own experience through the received texts, incarnating its symbolic level of meaning in new social and historical modes of living.

References

Aichele, G. (1997) *Text, Sign and Scripture* (Sheffield: Sheffield Academic Press).

Alter R. and Kermode, F. (1987) *The Literary Guide to the Bible* (London: Fontana).

Auld, G. (1994) *Kings Without Privilege* (Edinburgh: T & T Clark).

Auld, G. (1996) 'Re-reading Samuel (historically): "Etwas mehr Nicht-wissen"' in Fritz and Davies (eds) (1996).

Bach, A. (1997) *Women, Seduction and Betrayal in Biblical Narrative* (Cambridge: Cambridge University Press).

Bar-Efrat, S. (1989) *Narrative Art in the Hebrew Bible* (2nd edn; Sheffield: Sheffield Academic Press).

Barstad, H. M. (1997) 'History and the Hebrew Bible' in Grabbe (ed.) (1997).

Bartlett, J. R. (ed.) (1997) *Archaeology and Biblical Interpretation* (London: Routledge).

Beal, T. K. and Gunn, D. (eds) (1997) *Reading Bibles, Writing Bodies* (London: Routledge).

Becking, B. (1997) 'Inscribed seals as evidence for Biblical Israel? Jeremiah 40:7–41:15 *par exemple*' in Grabbe (ed.) (1997).

The Bible Collective (1995) *The Post Modern Bible* (New Haven: Yale University Press).

Bowman, R. G. (1995) 'Narrative criticism of Judges: human purpose in conflict with divine presence' in Yee (ed.) (1995).

Brueggemann, W. (1992) *Old Testament Theology* (Minneapolis: Fortress Press).

Brueggemann, W. (1994) *A Social Reading of the Old Testament* (Minneapolis: Fortress Press).

Chalcroft, D. J. (ed.) (1997) *Social Scientific Old Testament Criticism* (Sheffield: Sheffield Academic Press).

Cross, F. M. (1973) *Canaanite Myth and Hebrew Epic* (Cambridge, MA: Harvard University Press).

Cryer, F. (1994) *Divination in Ancient Israel and its Ancient Near-Eastern Environment* (Sheffield: Sheffield Academic Press).

Davies, P. R. (1992) *In Search of Ancient Israel* (Sheffield: Sheffield Academic Press).

Dever, W. (1997) 'Archaeology and the emergence of Israel' in Bartlett (ed.) (1997).

Dumbrell, W. J. (1997) ' "In those days there was no king in Israel: Every man did what was right in his own eyes:" The purpose of the book of Judges reconsidered' in Exum (ed.) (1997).

Edelman, D. (ed.) (1995) *The Triumph of Elohim* (Kampen: Kok Pharos).

Edelman, D. (1996) 'Saul ben Kish in history and tradition' in Fritz and Davies (eds) (1996).

Eilberg-Schwartz, H. (1997) 'The problem of the body for the People of the Book' in Beal and Gunn (eds) (1997).

Elazar, D. J. (1995) *Covenant and Polity in Biblical Israel* (New Brunswick and London: Transaction Press).

Exum, C. (1992) *Tragedy and Biblical Narrative* (Cambridge: Cambridge University Press).

Exum, C. (1996) *Plotted, Shot and Painted* (Sheffield: Sheffield Academic Press).

Exum, C. (ed.) (1997) *The Historical Books* (Sheffield: Sheffield Academic Press).

Finkelstein, I. (1988) *The Archaeology of the Israelite Settlement* (Jerusalem: Israel Exploration Society).

Flanagan, J. (1997) 'Chiefs in Israel' in Chalcroft (ed.) (1997).

Fritz, V. (1994) *An Introduction to Biblical Archaeology* (Sheffield: Sheffield Academic Press).

Fritz, V. (1995) *The City in Ancient Israel* (Sheffield: Sheffield Academic Press).

Fritz, V. (1996) 'Monarchy and re-urbanisation: a new look at Solomon's kingdom' in Fritz and Davies (eds) (1996).

Fritz, V. and Davies, P. R. (eds) (1996) *The Origins of the Ancient Israelite States* (Sheffield: Sheffield Academic Press).

Garbini, G. (1988) *History and Ideology in Ancient Israel* (London: SCM).

George, M. K. (1997) 'Assuming the body of the heir apparent: David's lament' in Beal and Gunn (eds) (1997).

Gnuse, R. (1997) *No Other Gods: Emergent Monotheism in Israel* (Sheffield: Sheffield Academic Press).

Gottwald, N. (1979) *The Tribes of Yahweh: A Sociology of the Religion of Liberated Israel* (Maryknoll, NY: Orbis).

Grabbe, L. (ed.) (1997) *Can a 'History of Israel' Be Written?* (Sheffield: Sheffield Academic Press).

Greenspahn, F. (ed.) (1991) *Essential Papers on Israel and the Ancient Near East* (New York: New York University Press).

Gunn, D. and Fewell, D. N. (1993) *Narrative Art in the Hebrew Bible* (Oxford: Oxford University Press).

Hawk, J. L. (1997) 'The problem with pagans' in Beal and Gunn (eds) (1997).

Jamieson-Drake, D. W. (1991) *Scribes and Schools in Monarchic Judah* (Sheffield: Sheffield Academic Press).

Laffey, A. L. (1988) *Wives, Harlots and Concubines* (London: SPCK).

Lemche, N. P. (1988) *Ancient Israel* (Sheffield: Sheffield Academic Press).

Longman III, T. and Reid, D. G. (1995) *God Is a Warrior* (Carlisle: Paternoster).

Mason, R. (1997) *Propaganda and Subversion in the Old Testament* (London: SPCK).

Mayes, A. D. H. (1985) *Judges* (Sheffield: Sheffield Academic Press).

Meyers, C. (1997) 'The family in ancient Israel' in Perdue, Blenkinsopp, Collins and Meyers (1997).

McConville, G. (1993) *Grace in the End* (Carlisle: Paternoster).

McConville, G. and Millar, J. G. (1994) *Time and Place in Deuteronomy* (Sheffield: Sheffield Academic Press).

Miles, J. (1995) *God: A Biography* (New York: Simon & Schuster).

Moran, W. L. (1991) 'The ancient near-eastern background of the love of God in Deuteronomy' in Greenspahn (ed.) (1991).

Niditch, S. (1993) *War in the Hebrew Bible* (Oxford: Oxford University Press).

Nielsen, F. A. J. (1997) *The Tragedy in History* (Sheffield: Sheffield Academic Press).

Noth, M. (1981 edn) *The Deuteronomistic History* (Sheffield: Sheffield Academic Press).

Noth, M. (1960) *The History of Israel* (2nd edn; London: A. & C. Black; reissued London: Xpress Reprints, 1996).

Overholt, T. (1996) *Cultural Anthroplogy and the Old Testament* (Minneapolis: Fortress Press).

Perdue, L. G., Blenkinsopp, J., Collins, J. J. and Meyers, C. (1997) *Families in Ancient Israel* (Louisville: Westminster John Knox).

Preston, T. (1997) 'The heroism of Saul: the pattern of meaning in the narrative of early kingship', in Exum (ed.) (1997).

Rowlett, L. (1997) 'Inclusion, exclusion and marginality in the book of Joshua' in Exum (ed.) (1997).

Saggs, H. W. F. (1991) 'The Divine in history', in Greenspahn (ed.) (1991).

Schafer-Lichtenberger, C. (1996) 'Sociological and biblical views of the early state' in Fritz and Davies (eds) (1996).

Schmidt, B. B. (1995) 'The aniconic tradition: on reading images and viewing text' in Edelman (ed.) (1995).

Steiner, G. (1961) *The Death of Tragedy* (London: Faber & Faber).

Thompson, H. O. (1987) *Biblical Archaeology* (New York: Paragon House).

Walsh, J. T. (1996) *I Kings* (Collegeville, MN: Glazier).

Whitelam, K. (1996) *The Invention of Ancient Israel* (London: Routledge).

Yee, G. (ed.) (1995) *Judges and Method* (Minneapolis: Fortress Press).

Younger, K. L. (1990) *Ancient Conquest Accounts. A Study in Ancient Near-Eastern and Biblical History* (Sheffield: Sheffield Academic Press).

Index